THE WORLD'S LEADING INTERNET MARKETERS

GLOBAL
PUBLISHING
GROUP

Global Publishing Group
Australia • New Zealand • Singapore • America • London

THE WORLD'S LEADING INTERNET MARKETERS

How Ordinary People
Make Extraordinary Money Online

DAVID LEE
DARREN J STEPHENS & DAVID CAVANAGH

First Edition 2011

Copyright © 2011 by Stephens, Darren, 1964 & Cavanagh, David, 1965

National Library of Australia
Cataloguing-in-Publication entry:

The World's Leading Internet Marketers

1st ed.
ISBN: 9781921630736 (pbk.)

Published by Global Publishing Group
PO Box 517 Mt Evelyn, Victoria 3796 Australia
Email info@TheGlobalPublishingGroup.com

For Further information about orders:
Phone: +61 3 9736 1156 or Fax +61 3 8648 6871

I dedicate this book to those that believe they can change the world for better, but are searching for a place to start. Opportunity doesn't knock on the door while sitting back watching a favourite TV show. Life, when you live it, is far more fulfilling when you become the show and being the people's favourite channel.

You can achieve if you believe you can. They say we are just 6 degrees of separation from any person we want to connect to on the planet. You will know you are on the right path when you see that number count down one-by-one. It may not happen immediately, but you will understand what I mean as it happens. No one is out of reach!

This book will open your eyes to the technological revolution that may well be leaving you and your business behind in its wake. Today's tough economic times are even more reason not to bury your head in the sand, but to use this technology to discover new business opportunities globally, and not just in your neighbourhood or within your national borders.

David Lee

We dedicate this book to all the people who dare to dream and who have the courage, persistence and commitment to take action to achieve those dreams.

Darren Stephens & David Cavanagh

Acknowledgements

It has been an honour and privilege to write this book. As with any major project, there are a number of very special people who contributed to making this book happen. So, I'd like to take this opportunity to say "THANK YOU".

Firstly, I'd like to thank my Co Authors Darren Stephens & David Cavanagh who were the inspiration for this book.

A special Thank You to the Amazing Companies featured in this book. Your willingness to share your secrets is a priceless gift. It has been an honour and a tremendous privilege to work with every one of you and I'm sure that thousands of people's lives will be influenced by the stories and insights that you've shared.

Next, I would like to thank my peers in the industry who believed 100% in me reaching my goals when sometimes it seemed like light-years away. That includes my co-author, David Cavanagh, who remained positive throughout, and later introduced me to Darren Stephens, making this collaboration possible.

My life quote is "Start small, THINK BIG!" I could never imagine the business associates I have today compared to a few years ago. I don't say that they are better as people, but they too share the same dream to achieve to their potential and even beyond.

To Narelle Urbanowicz for her brilliant graphic work and patience for all the ongoing changes....thanks for your flexibility!

A huge Thank You to our publisher Global Publishing Group and to their Awesome team, Jackie Tallentyre, Lesley Johnson, Michelle Tallentyre & Sonia Vasey. To Joel Fulton & the team at Dennis Jones & Associates for your dedication and commitment to the book's success.

Lastly, but most importantly, I would like to thank my dearest supporter and wife, Sabera, who believed in me, without always understanding where I was taking us. When friends and family questioned the business they couldn't see with their own eyes, you didn't waiver in your belief in me one little bit. Doing things differently is not always generally understood, but the most satisfying part of success is sharing it with those that stood by you all along, and that included our sons Gerard and Adrian.

EXTRA BONUSES!!

We can't give you everything you need to know about becoming Rich and Successful in one small book.

So we've created lots of extra special goodies, just for you. You'll find lots of money making Bonuses that will help fast track your success. There is FREE Live training & online resources to help you to grow your business and success. There's even downloadable videos.

Go check out our resources and FREE success tools NOW at:

www.TheCashFlowInvestor.com/livetraining

www.darrenjstephens.com/free-gifts-richard-branson/

www.BestCoachingProgram.com/giftbonus

Table of Contents

> *It's in moments of decision your destiny is created.*

Darren J Stephens

International Bestselling Author & Speaker

020 862 61880   8.00am Register

Introduction
Welcome to the Internet "Gold Rush"

The Internet has revolutionised the way the world lives, communicates and does business. It has opened doors that have never before been open and provided people with opportunities that have never existed before. For some this Internet revolution has been a simple way to communicate and get along and for others it has become a way of utilising a digital golf rush.

Like the printing press before it, the Internet revolution changed the way that people read, wrote and learned. It altered the perceptions of the ways we connect, and is continuing to bring the world closer together. Now, neighbors in Shanghai and Rio de Janeiro might be closer than two neighbors living right next to each other.

For some, it has been a way to connect with grandkids living across the country; for others, a simple way to do business remotely from their own home offices; or for others still, the Internet has existed as a way to shop, a way to learn directions, a way to get news and a way to stay in tune with the latest media and entertainment.

But, for a growing segment of the population, the Internet has excelled as a way to make a living. The money making possibilities on the Internet are now fully coming into being, and into full recognition, and people are recognising more than ever the ways to make money with this massive marketing, advertising and retailing tool.

The Internet has become a main method of marketing for both individuals and businesses around the world and this method allows them to reach a massive audience that is bigger than ever.

With the free to access waves of the Internet, browsers, surfers and website junkies can happen upon any website in their search for products, goods and services, and this means that any business with an Internet presence is in play here.

The Internet revolution has not entirely propagated itself, and we are here to show you why the changes in technology, overall, have made for a marketing gold rush, and how all of these changes are leading to a phenomenon in Internet money making.

Changes in Technology

It is not only the advent and explosion of the Internet that is propagating the growth in sales, marketing and advertising on the Internet, but the technology that has made the Internet mobile and more accessible than ever.

Smart phones, notebooks and tablets are making the Internet on the go more realistic, and all of these changes have combined to make making money not only possible, but realistic for many people.

Now, with an iPhone, Android or Blackberry, you can access wireless networks from anywhere within your network's range. This capability allows you to connect with all of your marketing and advertising endeavors online – and all at any time of the day.

With an iPhone in your pocket, you can shoot off emails anytime, add a post to your blog, make an eBay purchase or even transfer money. There are applications that allow you to specifically alter your blog content, others that give you the chance to track your Google AdWords, and still others that let you customise your website pages.

With a small touch screen device, you can type massive amounts of content into your webpage and contact followers, consumers, customers and clients from anywhere. You can even use these multimedia phones to add pictures and videos to your blog, website or YouTube account. You can record your voice, use automatic text message or complete email marketing campaigns from your favorite coffee house, your vacation cabin or even walking down a busy street.

Furthermore, products like Apple's iPad give you the chance to further your business model with an even easier to use interface. The larger screen, light weight and easy navigation features can have you accessing any of your business websites online, all without the use of a laptop – let alone a desktop computer.

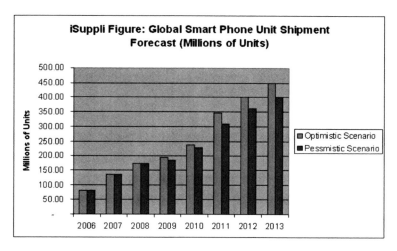

With this growing use of cell phones, the ability to stay digitally attached at all times is essential to running a business in a short attention span world. You must stay connected at all times, and having this smart mobile technology is one of the most essential things you can do. Having the technology, mastering it and allowing it to run every type of transaction you complete with your Internet business will not only be important, but may make or break your gold rush ideology.

This wireless revolution is not only changing how we communicate, but is also altering the way that we do business around the world. You can order content online, send payments and even search out products and clients online.

It is changing even the way traditional businesses advertise. Companies are beginning to use all sorts of wireless methods to communicate with their customers, and these methods are replacing even the most well-trusted means of contacting people.

Text message alerts can be signed up for, automatic emails can be sent, and these are replacing the need for newspaper advertisements, direct mail campaigns and even postcards and coupons. With the changing technology of social media, people and businesses can now contact you on your Twitter feed, your Facebook page, your MySpace profile or any of a number of other social networking sites and tools.

It is essential to know the ins and outs of these tools and to understand how to contact your clients and customers. You need to optimise these resources to reach more customers than ever before, and give yourself the opportunity to market yourself for free to a larger base of customers than you ever have before.

Facebook has expanded to hundreds of millions of users and now occupies the number two slot on the most visited webpage list. The only site ahead of it, Google, also allows you to market yourself cheaply and reach in the range of many hundreds of millions of users, all without needing manpower, without spending a lot of money and without ever leaving your office.

Businesses are increasingly turning to these resources, and Facebook is no longer seen as the realm of only high schools and college kids. With an Oscar-nominated movie about the networking site, it is now taken seriously by all, and owners realise that the capabilities of this site can be indispensable for businesses of any kind. The marketing, advertising, buying and selling abilities cannot be taken lightly, and it is through these outlets that the marketing of the future is presenting itself.

Google, like Facebook, is used by millions of Internet viewers everyday, and represents the main method of gathering information for people all around the world. With Google, web-searchers have the ability to find anything online. Whether they are looking for clients, customers, consumers or businesses, Google will direct them to the ones in their area.

With Google searches you can position yourself to be placed at the top of search engine results by optimising your page in the correct way. When optimised, your pages will achieve the best results, make the most money and produce the most sales and contacts from potential customers and clients.

These methods are changing the way that we do business as a whole. Industries are now shying away from television and print advertisements, and placing them online more than ever. As people are now going to the Internet to watch TV, get their newspapers, see their video news, shop and look for entertainment, advertising space online is now at a premium.

While advertising spots can be purchased online on the largest and most visited sites, you can also find cheap or free ads that can be specialised on pages like Facebook or Google. With the right methods, you can place yourself in the best position to be presented to people that are looking for services or products similar to yours.

Business is now transacted on the computer more than ever before, and with this explosion of computer and Internet use, it is easy to understand how people are making so much money online.

Internet markets allow you to earn passive income as well as normal income, and you can use your website to sell products, to promote your physical business or to attract viewers to your brand. Even a simple blog with nothing to sell can make you money as you attract more and more viewers and you gain more and more clicks on your site.

If your site becomes a leader in your niche, you will likely have a large following and be attracting thousands of clicks everyday. If this is the case, people will pay to advertise their products on your page.

Facebook is just one of the sites that are changing the way that people do business. In addition to the fact that it is one of the largest, and quickest growing, websites on the Internet, it also provides tools and opportunities for business and money-making that are like few other opportunities.

Because Facebook is free to use, it allows for a free advertising program that can touch thousands to millions of people every day. With Facebook you can gain followers, create a fan page and encourage thousands of people to "Like" your page. Once people are following you on Facebook, you will have automatic access to their Facebook pages. You will be able to post to your wall, and it will show up on their feeds. If you bring specific customers into your comments, you can expand to specified customers and areas even more easily.

Using Facebook, you can link to a Twitter page or promote your blogs and websites as well. These opportunities are like few others on the Web and allow you to create unique content, share whatever content you would, and do it all in a way that is succinct, concise and easy to navigate.

This guide will allow you to discover the ways that the Internet is changing the business world and how it can spell a new beginning for you in your life. This is your blueprint to making money online and, hey, if you're one of the lucky and dedicated ones, you can become one of those Internet millionaires you have always dreamed of becoming.
Wishing you every success !

Cheers
David Lee, Darren & David

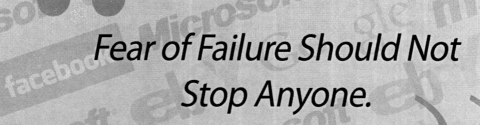

> # *Fear of Failure Should Not Stop Anyone.*

Larry Page

Google Founder - Billionaire

CHAPTER 1

The Internet Revolution
The Keys to Online Marketing

Chapter 1
The Internet Revolution

This chapter will give you an overview of the basic concepts that will be covered in more detail later in the book.

The Keys to Online Marketing

You should always know what you are doing before you begin it, and this starts with a foolproof business plan. You should not simply ride a bandwagon, but know how to do what you are doing and fully understand it. Have a goal in mind and stick with it.

1) Stick to what feels good

   Don't be tied to any single method when completing your Internet marketing. Know what you are doing and keep yourself attached to what feels right and what feels like it is working.

2) Know that your prospects and customers are looking for the right information

   Prospects will not be deterred; they will eventually find a source of information that they like and they will continue looking until they do. So remain steadfast in your site, because there is a market for a real professional.

3) Content is king

   You've heard it before, but the old idiom remains true. The pages on your website and the information you are supplying is essential to drawing business.

4) Embrace yourself as editor

Don't just write your website and leave. Keep up with the site and make the changes that are necessary to improve it whenever possible.

5) Become an expert, not an advertiser

Most people do not trust simple advertising, but they will trust someone who is truly a master of their craft. You need to know the right way to sell yourself as an expert, and the only way is by truly having expert content.

6) Community

Build a fan base and list of visitors that will keep coming back to you. This is business 101. Know how to attract visitors and keep them coming back for your expertise and the high quality of your content.

> ### *"Build a fan base and list of visitors that will keep coming back to you."*

Attract, Convert, Transform

The key to moving from a one man business to a digital marketing enterprise, these three steps will have you attracting clients from across the globe.

To attract customers and clients, you need a great brand, outcome and differentiator.

Brand – Your brand needs to be easily identifiable. It needs to have a certain attitude and be described in just one word.

Outcome – You need not describe your process to your clients, but you need to show them the end product the goods.

Differentiator – You also need something that sets you apart in your industry. You need something to make you shine above all others in your field. You need to know your competition, and go above and beyond them to excel at your business.

With the steps listed below, you can utilise the following to attract customers:

> Blogging
> Social media networking
> Articles
> SEO content
> Videos
> Giveaways
> Joint Ventures
> Social bookmarking

If this is too much for you to keep up with, you can start by simply selecting two and doing them well. Which leads to the next step…

Educate, Market and Sell

Your website should be used to educate others about your process, tell them why your website is special and sell them on buying your products.

The information you provide on your website is essentially your product and you must make the visitors want to consume your information.

Not every single person who visits your website, reads your newsletters or downloads your articles will want to buy your products or come back for your information.

Although not all of these people will become clients, there is a chance they will tell friends or family about your website and this will attract others to your goods or services.

Catering to Consumers and Would-Be Clients

You have to convert the would-be clients to actual consumers and customers. If you have a client signed up to your eZine, you need them to visit your website and buy your products.

The next step in the process is transforming. You have to transform your potential client into an actual customer. This can be done by delivering on your services and promises, and even over-delivering.

Many may think the process takes a long time, but this is not always the case. The process can be completed quickly by setting up the system and putting it on auto pilot.

In one scenario, your clients may visit your Facebook page and this may in turn lead them to signing up to your eZine. In this case, you can then continue to cultivate a relationship with a client as they dig deeper into your product, and they eventually will purchase your goods or services.

With the advent of the Internet, you can move thousands of prospects almost instantaneously.

Grab and Keep People's Attention

With the amount of information available on the Internet, people can get overloaded with drab content and with articles and pages that simply fail to deliver anything useful.

Because this is the case, making your content of the highest quality will appeal to any visitor on the web. Your web pages should provide people with information that they cannot get elsewhere, and products and facts that visitors will find especially useful or entertaining.

Because experts are natural attention magnets, people will flock to someone who is proficient in their field. They will be interested in what someone has to say if they have established themselves as in the know and the authority on a product or service.

Shorter Sales Cycles

As an expert in your field, you will also enjoy the benefit of shorter sales cycles. People who come to you will require less research, and will push more people to your product. They will approach your site with confidence and you will find them buying quicker than ever.

Joint Ventures

Becoming an expert will also influence others in the trade to seek you out. They will look to connect with you because of your money making potential and, whether they are offering similar or complimentary products, it will enhance business.

> *"Becoming an expert will also influence others in the trade to seek you out."*

The Basics

The basics steps of leveraging the Internet must be understood before the technical ones, and these following steps will serve as the foundation of your sales approach.

Step 1 – Be Giving

Having the right attitude on your website is essential for making progress with your page. You need to cultivate an attitude of giving and gift your followers with free samples, free information and free facts and specials.

Step 2 – Relate to the Customers

Your customers and clients should know that you feel their pain and you should position yourself to explain their situation in your own words. Indicate that you have gone through the same things and provide the solutions that worked for you. Explain how you are the same and explain how the same tactics will work for them.

Step 3 – Branding

You should be able to brand your product in just one word or phrase. This is partly important because of the search tendencies of the Internet age, but it should also help consumers to identify you in a simple and concise way. The one word or one phrase brand would allow you to exude the essence of your business without any distractions to your brand.

Step 4 – Conveying Your Vision

Now that you are branded with keywords or key phrases, make sure that the vision of your brand or company is defined as well. Decide on an outcome that you can consistently deliver on. Just like a pizza place promising to deliver in less than 30 minutes or a group telling you that they are a one stop shop for anything, you should be able to convey your vision in a short paragraph or easily on your homepage.

These are, in essence, the basics to marketing your brand and producing your successful webpage. With these basics in mind, you can now move on to the more technical steps.

Step 5 – Ultimate Communication

With your brand established, you need then to determine how you are going to communicate this brand with the world. The premium ways to communicate your brand are online and the beauty of online communication lies in the multiple ways to convey the same or similar messages or ideas.

Ways to communicate your message include:

Online videos
Online newsletters
Blogs
Podcasts
Online forums
Social media sites
Wikis
White papers
Public relations
SEO articles
Webinars

Some may think that websites should be listed among these communication channels; however, your website generally will not receive as heavy traffic as other communication channels. Your other avenues of communication will garner traffic, which will then be driven to your website.

Picking a Domain Name

The domain name for your business is essential to your traffic. If should feature a short name, but should not sacrifice what you are trying to convey. Your domain name should be registered for three months or more, as most sites that are newer can be confused as spamming sites.

You need to find a server that allows you to pay a cheap fee every month and one that will give you the opportunity to host unlimited email addresses and domain names.

> *"The domain name for your business is essential to your traffic."*

Professional Design

All of the technical aspects of your site should be outsourced to a professional as the design of your site can make or break your business. The design of your site should be done from the perspective of converting leads into sales as well as with an eye for color and style. Just like your real life home, you wouldn't take on the project yourself – it is best left to someone with experience.

Website Navigation

Navigating your website should be a process that will not leave others in confusion. Visitors, consumers and clients should be able to find themselves on your page, and locate all of the essentials without having to worry about clicking a dozen times or going through unnecessary contact pages.

Creating Content

Content, as the saying goes, is king. And this is no different for your website. You need to establish your brand with one word, come up with your vision and define the problem that you are trying to solve. All of these steps will help you with the next step: trying to produce excellent content for your visitors. You need to determine the following things:

What are you offering?
Who are you trying to reach?
Who have you helped and where is the proof?
What is your company all about and why is it credible?

Traffic

The last step, and perhaps the most important, is driving the traffic to your actual website.

Link from other Sites

Linking from other sites will allow you to reap the rewards of the visitors on other pages. You can link your site to blogs and forums, and drive these visitors to your page in droves.

Submit Articles

Submitting articles will give you the opportunity to get some of your expertise onto the Internet, and leave customers wanting more.

Social Media and Bookmarking

One of the most popular traffic-driving methods on the Internet, social media like Facebook and Twitter allows you to reach visitors without any effort. You can freely post your pages on sites like StumbleUpon, Digg and Reddit.

Your page needs to attract visitors and, as we've stated, the best way to do this is with blogs, eZines and social media sites. Your website is worthless unless it gets visitors and these methods help to attract visitors.

You need to keep your content to a certain quality standard, as one time visitors will not help you. You need people coming back and people giving good reviews of your site.

The Internet is one of the best ways to stay connected and, if people like what they are seeing on your website, they may take the small amount of time to email the site or send it along in a tweet or Facebook post.

eZines

eZines are one way of attracting customers and allow you to deliver emails and newsletters in the form of an article.

Search Engine Optimisation (SEO)

In the not so recent past of ink and paper, businesses could easily market themselves to a whole new population of customers by spending their money on things like print advertisements. With the Yellow Pages, newspaper, TV advertisements, the radio, direct mail and the early days of the Internet, marketing was pretty straightforward. Now, in a wireless and modernised marketplace, one of the few advertising mediums seeing results is the Internet. To understand why, you should first take a look at the other mediums, to learn how we arrived at this point.

At the present it is like having just one phone book to advertise, except that phone book is no longer the Yellow Pages, but Google. Nearly every person using the Internet is seeing the ads on Google, and making your ad the top of the page is a top priority for everyone.

What is SEO?

Describing SEO can be thought of in the same terms as your personal credit score. If you were searching for your credit score today, each of the three main reporting agencies would provide you with separate scores and numbers. These numbers are calculated using different algorithms, and so the numbers would never be exactly the same. Likewise, Google, Yahoo and MSN feature different algorithms for placing websites at the top of their search listings. If you are a mechanic from San Diego, and a user types "San Diego mechanic" into their search engine, and your website is listed at the top of the search results, you will have received the highest ranking from that search engine.

If you show up on page two, on the other hand, it will be because your score was not high enough. If you type in "San Diego auto repair" and you show up as the eighth spot on page one, as opposed to page two for the "mechanic" search, that will mean that your ranking for the second term was higher than the first term.

An important consideration when dealing with SEO regards your target audience. The search engines like to think of themselves as all-encompassing dictionary and encyclopedia services, as well as directory and phone books, and their chief goal is to keep their users happy. In order to keep their users happy, they need to supply them with the best information. This can only be done by keeping the information current, relevant and reliable. If people enter and exit your website (your bounce rate) in less than seven seconds, your pages will not be kept at the top of listings.

This is because Google will not deem your website content to be very valuable and it will not be recognised as what Google users are looking for. If a website is ugly, unprofessional or confusing web viewers will not stay long. They will look for a website that is professional, fun, easy and dedicated to providing something they need. The first page – the confusing and ugly one – will be difficult for a professional to optimise because of the amount of work that will be needed to get it to the point of the second page.

In other words, SEO is largely driven by fresh, unique content that providers users and visitors with valuable information that they are looking for.

How Does SEO Really Work?

SEO is short for search engine optimisation. It involves structuring your website's code and content so that it receives the highest possible ranking from the search engines and is a process that must constantly be tweaked and updated. This can be a difficult and confusing process as none of the engines are upfront about the way that their algorithms work and few are willing to tell exactly how to get the best rankings.

Much of the current SEO knowledge has been ascertained from trial and error. Companies like Noble Image have studied and observed the top ranking SEO products, and have been around since 1998, helping companies to optimise even the most difficult to market words and products. The big three search engines do not provide for users a guide on how to optimise their website in regard to search engine ranking, and this is to keep the number of favorable rankings from overwhelming the system. To Google, your page must be relevant to what people are searching for, and this will give it the best chance of ranking highly. If irrelevant or seedy results are populating the top pages, the search engine will lose customers to the next search engine, and they in turn will lose money.

> *"To Google, your page must be relevant to what people are searching for..."*

The Myth of SEO

Website design companies may present themselves as unique or difficult to find in an industry, but they truthfully are a dime a dozen. With the advent of the Internet it is possible for anyone who can learn HTML to compete in the design industry – and compete legitimately. Because SEO is becoming essential to the industry, design companies are increasingly advertising themselves as SEO experts and this is overestimating their capability to get you into the optimisation game and making money.

Ineffective SEO Strategies

1) **Cloaking**
   Do not allow your website to cloak its content by offering content that an engine spider will see but a human will not see.

2) **Invisible text**
   Do not add invisible text to your website to enhance keywords or links, as this can be detected by search engine spiders.

3) Hyphenated domain names
These should also be avoided as they will hurt your chances of acquiring the kind of type-in traffic that is essential for a high ranking.

4) Duplicate content
Duplicate content will bring about heavy penalties, in search engine rank, if you have multiple pages that are the same within one website.

5) Copying or plagiarising content
Not only is this illegal and unethical, but it will force you to be blocked from SEO engines altogether, and can result in legal problems.

6) Reciprocal linking
This type of SEO mistake will leave a search engine like Google looking back and forth between links to try to figure out which link has the authority.

7) Keyword stuffing
Putting too many keywords or keywords that are unrelated to your site on your pages can also hurt your rankings by setting up the opportunity to be banned or to lose your rankings.

8) Misspelling optimisation
This happens when you try to capitalise on misspelled searches by entering misspelled words on your page, in hope that visitors will match these searches. This can also negatively affect the search rankings from different engines.

9) Doorway pages
Doorway pages are not only annoying for users on your pages,

but they can also force the search engine spiders to search for your content and will result in your search rankings being hurt.

10) Using Flash as a doorway page

What was once used as a focal point in many doorway pages, Flash can now hurt your rankings as some search engines will skip over the doorway, not even taking your hard work into account.

11) Using Flash as a primary navigation tool

Again, Flash is often not even considered by search engine spiders, and these flash features will be simply passed over by search engine spiders and optimisers.

12) Frames

Frames would allow you to assemble a website page from the code of several other pages. One page might be the header, another would be the navigation bar and another would be the content. Although modern spiders understand they should see this collage as one page, it's still confusing to interpret. Making these pages, as a web designer, is no fun either. Stay away from frames; you'll never need them if you know what you're doing.

Summary

As you can see, there are a number of steps involved in creating your own millionaire Internet business. Now that you have an overview of the basics and a view of the big picture it's time to get down to specifics.

> *It is Our Choices....That Show What We Truly Are, Far More Than Our Abilities.*

J.K.Rowling

International Bestselling Author

CHAPTER 2

Doing Research to
Find a Niche Market

Chapter 2
Doing Research to Find a Niche Market

From a practical point of view, finding a niche is an exercise in brainstorming and logic, self reflection and online research.

Write Down a List of Your Hobbies and Interests

Review your hobbies, passions and interests from day to day and weeks to week – all the things that you have studied, lived and experienced.

Have you traveled overseas? Do you collect something, or participate in a sport or club? Have you worked in a particular area that you know really well? Do you have a strong desire to learn something new?

If this list of passions can not produce the topic of a niche, expand and go beyond your passions to other people's passions. Search the Internet.

Delve into stores like Amazon.com and auction sites and marketplaces like eBay.com. These sites will provide you a population of millions of users, and these users will give you millions of ideas for a blog topic. Amazon and eBay make so much money because they offer so much to so many people. It is your job to find out what it is that these people are pursuing the most often, and give it to them. Don't stop at Amazon, try Yahoo Shopping and Google Product Search. Browse through magazines racks, which are – in their essence – a rack of niches people have proven to be interested in.

A fantastic way to find niches that will earn you money and give you something to write about, these topics have already been proven as profitable because they exist so successfully offline.

You could also explore what bloggers have used and what is making money for them across the internet, and adopt ideas like these, ideas similar to these or ideas complimentary to these.

All of these markets and marketplaces will break down from their large offering of products into smaller niches. The niches all carry different degrees of demand, and those with high demand have different areas that cater to more specialised consumers and providers. There is no reason why you cannot focus on just one aspect of a broad topic.

For instance, you could use the following:

- Instead of "Exotic food" use "Exotic Indian Food"
- Instead of "Sports Cars" use "Foreign Sports Cars"
- Instead of "Clothes" use "Women's Clothes"

Topics like these can be broken down once, and then broken down again and again as long as the topic is broad enough to draw an audience still. Breaking your topic down will allow you to attract a more specific audience.

Should You Concentrate on What You Enjoy?

As with any money-making plan, there are annals of advice out there, dictating how to do this or how to do that. In this case, there is a multitude of advice about the correct way to choose a topic to blog about.

Some will say to focus on what will drive the most traffic and produce the most profit. They will say to find a niche that people are spending money on, lots of money, and the ones that are not faced with stiff competition.

Others will tell you not to worry about the profit. They will say to find something that you are invested in – something that you are passionate about – and blog about that. They will tell you to make your niche there and enjoy and be knowledgeable about your subject. There will come a motivation and satisfaction outside of profit that will hopefully drive profit. Your ability to create quality content on this kind of subject will be higher.

While either piece of advice can be viewed as valid, there is no right answer. Perhaps the best method would be to combine the best parts of the two methods.

While the process motivates some, the topic motivates others. Why not be motivated be both, and combine your passions with your profits?

CHAPTER 3

Developing Your Own
eBusiness Model

Chapter 3
Developing Your Own eBusiness Model

When developing your business model, the first thing you need to consider is the demand for your product. You need to decide if your business will be capable of getting off the ground, or you need to create your own demand for the product. While creating demand will not be for the light hearted or for the beginner, finding a profitable niche may not be as hard.

As is mentioned in the last chapter, once you find your niche, you will be positioned to develop your online eBusiness model. You will then have to identify the scalability of your product. You should determine what you can sell, or how much you can sell, at the back (or low) end of the market, and use this information to determine where you will make most of your money.

You will either have to find a niche where you can continually sell to the same customers, or where you can attain a large client base. Selling to the same customers will allow you to make more money with less effort, though this may be less feasible. You need to know the types of businesses you will be competing against, and gauge their profits against your profitability.

Realise that your business may not all come from one type of transaction. If your business is a dog training company, you should realise that you can also sell product online to complement the training, or even sell dog-grooming services or dog-food products. You can then save your customers time and effort by offering these other add on services.

The main aspect of your competitiveness in the market will be determined largely by your prices. You need to know that undercutting works, but it may not be the best tactic for your business. You need to look at how much your product or service costs and what influence it has on your customers.

Know the value of your product before determining your price and then set it against the values and prices of products from your competitors. To be able to increase your price, you need to establish your company as an authority in your particular niche, product or service. You need to know how to beat everyone else, whether this is in price or quality, or a combination of the two, and you have to give yourself a chance to sell as much as possible.

Branding

You then need to decide whether you are marketing yourself or the company. Some people market themselves individually, while many others use their eBusiness to market their product or service from a company perspective. If you create the brand around yourself, you may be limiting the life expectancy of your company and may not leave yourself with the opportunity to sell the company or allow your children to profit from it.

Building the Model

Brainstorming is an essential first step of building and developing your eBusiness, and it is one that should not be overlooked in any circumstance. Even if you think you know your business, product or service, planning is an essential step of the process. In every step of developing your business, you should write down all of the ideas that you may have. This is your opportunity to go wild when determining what you are trying to do, and you should put yourself in the position to think as big as possible. You can edit all of these ideas later, but you should use this situation to commit them all to paper.

Once you are done getting out all of your ideas, you then need to structure them into a format that gives you the best chance of success. You need to determine what aspects should be considered further and which ones can be scaled with your business. While you are not starting yet, or committing to anything, this is essential research that will get your business model off the ground.

You can also research your ideas by using the Google Keywords tools and this will give you an opportunity to check and see what the demand is for each of your ideas. You can decide in which ways you will be competitive and you can then determine what products, ideas and services are selling the best.

The Process

The process begins after the initial brainstorming, and you will have to accomplish three things after this. You will first have to build a product, build a list of devoted customers that are into your specialised niche and then develop a relationship with the people that are willing to engage in buying your products or services.

While it may seem like that is all there is to it, this may not be the easiest process. Another part of this process is getting people to like and trust you, and getting them to buy your products,

Decide on Your Product

The next step in your business model will be selecting your product. You may already have a business, or you may have already established your niche, so this will not apply to you. Also, you may think that because you are not selling anything physical, you do not have to pick out a product, but having additional products can be extremely worthwhile.

The process of deciding what product you will sell is partially determined when you select your niche, as this decision guides you as to what products you may choose to offer. It will take a little bit of foresight to plan future products and to put yourself in the position to maximise the sales process. If you are solely running your business online, things will be different, but if you are running a concurrent offline business, you will know how to apply and supply the specialist knowledge, and you must determine how this will translate to your online product.

Without focusing too much on specifics, you have to be able to think laterally – it is essential that you give yourself the opportunity to use these general concepts to translate your different areas of business into the biggest earning capabilities possible.

You may choose to find which products are the easiest to create and gain a profit from, and look towards these first. At the bottom rung of this ladder, you will find text products. These may make you the least money, but are the fastest and easiest way of disseminating your knowledge and allowing your following to understand what it is that you are trying to convey.

There are five different types of products you can utilise in total, and these include the following:

Text Products

As already mentioned, text products are the easiest, fastest and cheapest of products, but they will likely provide for the smallest of profits. With text products, you may be at the lower end of your earnings scale, but you will be in a position where you have got the ball rolling and started things on the right foot.

One example of text products is an eBook. This type of content takes almost no investment, unless you are outsourcing to a professional, and even then it can be done relatively cheaply. If you are writing your own eBook, you have only to put all of your research and ideas about your topic onto paper, and write it all down in an organised format.

You can also create something called an e-course, which is a popular option for those running membership websites. This e-course can teach your followers or members how to do something and you can add the content of the e-course to a number of e-mails or direct messages, which then can be loaded to an auto-responder to be given directly to your client base, your list of customers, or even general visitors or sign-ups to your website.

These types of products are used to establish you as a trusted voice in the industry and they give you more credibility and a higher degree of authority. With your text products, you can either sell them or give them away, but they should always be among your lower cost products. You will be able to use these products to springboard into more expensive products and this will be essential for your business plan.

This is a great website to check out as it's normal kept a secret by internet marketers as it gives you the master resell rights or private label rights to products that are already created.

The website is www.UnselfishMarketer.com/Discount

You could have a free report on one small aspect of your business – you should make it instructional and all useful information, but only use it to scratch the surface. Once this report has generated interest for the product, you could then release a full sized book to further get into the topic. This will allow you to build trust, and to capitalise off your initial momentum generated by the free report. This can also be a popular way of building a list of potential prospects to whom you will be positioned to offer more promotions to at various points in the future.

Audio Products

While these will likely take more work than your eBooks or text products, an audio product will also not be very difficult to come by. It has a higher perceived value because of its format, and will likely allow you to charge a higher price than your simple text formats.

You can record a teleconference call with an expert in the field, you can record yourself giving a useful lesson or you can conduct a question and answer session using Skype. There are various options when determining how to release your audio files, and you can then translate or transcribe these into text files if necessary, allowing you to double your profits with the same product.

These can be done in a day or two, and audio podcasts will allow you to connect to your visitors more quickly than ever before. For example, if you were running a health clinic, you could interview a health expert, or give your own talk on practices and procedures, and simply post the audio file to the website – either free or for your users and members to purchase for a small price.

These methods will also help you to build your credibility, and they can be used to establish authority as well.

Video Products

Videos are a way of incorporating the most interesting content on your page and to get people interested and excited unlike any other form of product. Just like YouTube.com has enjoyed an incredible popularity, as well as Vevo.com, these tools can be used to address the short attention spans of users and followers.

For example, if you had a band you were promoting, place actual videos on your page of a performance or recent show. Film yourself traveling or goofing around, and allow your fans to connect to your band.

Your video content could be funny, shocking or exciting. Like the videos on YouTube that get the most views, odd or exciting content will get people laughing or gasping, and will drive visitors to your page in droves larger than ever before.

You can easily film your own videos with cameras, or even with your phone, and upload it to sites like YouTube. You can then click the 'Video" tab on your page and share these with your followers. These often produce the most comments and buzz from followers.

Like videos, you can also use links to create excitement for your page. The links should be, like all other content, useful or exciting. You should give your followers exclusive links to your products, links to articles about your brand or links to reviews of whatever you are doing.

These videos and these links will not only enhance your ability to help and reward your viewer and followers, but will give you the opportunity to share other content from across the Web. In addition to increasing the buzz on your page, you can also get people to buy from your other websites, to draw traffic to your blog or even to follow your Twitter page.

This kind of attention can only be gleaned from content that is highly original and exciting. The videos could be a direct plea to your Facebook followers and you can even use this method as a shameless ploy to get them to tell their friends to increase your likes.

Membership Sites

A membership site is a form of eBusiness model in which a customer will pay a fee, usually monthly or yearly, to receive information from you on a regular basis and to be given access to tools and resources you provide in relation to your niche. Often, all delivery of this material is done online and can mostly be automated. As will be discussed later, membership sites give you the chance to take advantage of recurring income. These sites give you the chance to get monthly income, and you can earn from a large base of visitors and members. With a membership site, even if visitors drop out after 3-4 months, you will still be earning money from new members and the people that have stayed on. And you will be doing the same amount of work as your clients increase. Whether you are making money from 10 members or from 100, you will be issuing the same content. So, although the work may not match the price at the beginning, it will expand greatly as your users start to grow exponentially.

Software Products

These can be the trickiest kind of products to sell and will likely force you to do much more work than any other product. They, however, can also be some of the highest selling and will allow you to reap the greatest rewards and profits. If you are creating software and it doesn't sell, the risk will be high as it may have been very expensive to come up with.

But, if you have a quality product and people are buying, the rewards will be high as you can charge large amounts for each piece of software sold. Before going down this road, you should have some experience in developing software, or you should make sure that you have a trusted professional to do the job at a fair price. It is all about leveraging results with price and you need to get the most quality you can for the least money possible, to generate the highest profits that you can squeeze out of the product.

Your software can be subscription based and monetised and you can offer it to the members at different levels of membership on your site for different prices. You will be able to do a number of things with this idea and it can be an outlet that may lead you to your highest profits ever.

CHAPTER 4

Blogging for Profit

Chapter 4
Blogging for Profit

Throughout this chapter you will learn how to create great content for your blog, how to drive traffic to it and how to monetise it. If blogging isn't your thing (and it might be by the end of this chapter!) keep in mind that many of the ways to drive traffic to and monetise a blog can be mapped across to any eBusiness website.

The first step in blogging for profit is choosing which topic you will blog on. Consider picking a few topics that you will look forward to blogging about – that you will be able to write about and sell easily – and find the one that will provide the most consumers and the least competition.

Covering topics that you enjoy will allow you to focus on the content and make money from it, before delving into other topics that you can run for more profit, whether you enjoy them as much or not.

Ways to bridge the gap between writing for writing's sake and writing for money – for profit and income – include affiliate promotions, such as product reviews, which allow you to earn affiliate commissions.

While enjoying your blogging and squeezing profit from it are your two goals in making your blog, forgetting the profit at the beginning may be your best bet at making that profit. Blog at the beginning because you enjoy it. Enjoy it because consistency is essential when starting your blog. Your profits will likely be slim to none your first couple of months, so it is important not to get discouraged while beginning your blog. Maintain consistency your first couple months – keep drawing traffic and providing content – even if you are not earning profit initially, because you will if you stick to it.

It is important to find something that you can sit and write about because of the intrinsic value or reward, because you may not be making more than pennies for as much as six months.

While it is important to be patient, it is not desirable to blog for a year without making the kind of money you deserve for the time that you put in.

Because of this, it is essential to consider your readers and consumers, and affiliates and advertisers. Are your readers the kind of people who will be buying products? Are your affiliates the kind of people that will pay to advertise on your site?

As little traffic will draw you little money into your account, knowing this fact ensures you that more traffic will draw you more money. All you need to do is devise a strategy to increase your traffic steadily and incrementally.

Build an audience and attract loyal readers, but at the same time make money. While it will be rewarding to have loyal friends, fans and followers, it will be doubly rewarding to earn money because of your efforts.

As there were passions behind your decision to begin the blogging adventure to begin with, so too there are passions and motivation behind your readers. You must understand why your readers are reading you, why they are staying with you and what their spending habits are.

Understand your readers the same way you would understand yourself. Put yourself in their shoes. Because you and your reader are both in the same position of being interested in your niche and your blog, ask yourself, "Would I purchase these products? Would I keep reading? What is my motivation for reading this site? Would I spend my money?"

Once you answer these questions, you will have a greater grasp on what to sell your readers, what to write for your readers and how to get the most out of your readers.

Being a good marketer is also a part of the process. Knowing what products to sell is only half of the battle as you need to know how to present and market them and how to offer them in the most appealing way possible for your customers and readers.

Content creation and monetisation is the name of the game and combining both into a euphoria of serving your readers and serving yourself is your ultimate goal of blogging.

Even if the topics that you are considering are covered by other bloggers, try to find just one aspect of your sub-niche and become the absolute authority on it.

These types of blogs become easier to make money from since they are specific and attract a much more specific audience and much more specific advertising base.

There are dozens, hundreds and thousands of areas out there to blog on, whether the topics are sub niches, broad niches, or any other kind of niche. Finding the right kind of niche is a matter of luck and of research. The only rule that should be followed, when blogging on a very popular topic, is to ensure that you do not provide any duplicated content, which will downgrade your level on many Google search rankings.

How to Gain Traffic to Your Blog

Directing traffic to your blog can be done in several different ways. These methods need not simply be used, they must have time invested into them – they have to be crafted to fit your site and they have to be mastered to maximise profits.

While it is seen as an easy way of making money, it is still work and you are still trying to earn revenue and turn a very nice profit, whether you're working from home or not.

Remember, articles should be written for traffic generation as well as submitted for content.

When writing your articles, keep in mind the following:

- The articles should be used to gain clicks for your website.
- Focus on grammar and spelling. The articles should be clear and concise and display the content of your site.
- Provide a catchy headline.
- Write with passion; you need to be invested in your niche.
- Your articles should not include sales statements at any cost.
- Make them between 300-1000 words.
- Use short paragraphs.
- Use titles and subheadings.
- Write in the third person.

-Mention your product, service, company or website.

-State what makes you different (and better) than other similar sites or webpages.

In addition to the above, include the following in your articles as it appeals to people, brings in more readers and keeps them coming back for more:

- Tell the reader what their problem is
- Tell the reader why they need your site
- Tell the reader why your approach is different
- Tell how you can solve their problem

How to Optimise Your Blog for the Search Engines

Half of your job is done when you set up your blog, establish your niche and determine how you will be monetising it. Now that you have this done, it is time to optimise your blog for the search engines that will be such a large part of determining how much money you make.

Optimising your blog page is done in two ways, both of which are essential to the process.

These ways are:
- On page optimisation
- Off page optimisation

On page optimisation is done by posting key phrases for specific pieces of content in your blogs and on your pages. You need to post the keywords into your blog and your title and tag them with these keywords.

The off page optimisation is done by linking your page with these keywords. When off page optimising, be sure to use keywords that will attract the most visitors to your site, and will give them exactly what they are looking for and what it says that you will be giving them.

The reasons to optimise your page include:

- More readers
- Higher ranking on search engines
- A higher crawling index
- More profits

The best ways to get incoming links to your page are as follows:

1. Links on your other blogs and pages

Links from your other blogs will give you the chance to have many crosslinks. Linking from blog to blog will let you earn money even when people are leaving your pages, because they will be moving from your pages to other pages run by you.

2. Links from submitting articles

Submitting articles to article directories will allow you to get more exposure for your content and allow you to link to your main page through all of these articles and sites.

One main article directory, www.articleassistance.com, allows you to automatically connect to around 150 article directories in only an hour, saving yourself as much as five hours of the time it would take for you to do it manually, page by page.

These article directories are a place for people to find your articles and will allow you to present them to as many people as possible.

Within a few days or a few weeks, these article directories and links will be sending dozens to hundreds to thousands of new viewers to your articles or pages because they are being found more easily than they ever were before.

Researching and writing an article in around 20-40 minutes can allow you to earn a large profit for your time through directories like these.

How to Get Your Blog Known

Your blog must become established as a valuable place for information and an interesting place for content before you begin worrying about it as a profitable and money-making tool or resource.

It is recommended to have at least ten pieces of strong and fresh content on your blog before your begin to monetise. These pieces, your ten pillar articles, will assist you to bring viewers in the first time they visit your site or click your page.

Without these pillar articles your visitors will leave the first time that they visit your site and they may not bother giving it a second chance.

Visitors have to be impressed with something compelling and if they are met with the right content, there is a higher chance that they will bookmark your page and check back to your site continually.

This quality content will allow you to form beneficial relationships with your visitors and will give you the benefit of having a site that people can trust and that they will be loyal to.

Simple trafficking techniques can be used at first to drive traffic to your site and create a buzz. After word gets around about your site, you can get serious about advertisements and monetisation.

Your best content should be set out – kind of like putting your best foot forward or making a good first impression – and optimised so that it is the first thing that most viewers will access.

Even if there is some poor content on your site, these pillar articles, that should be the easiest to find online, will allow users to get the kind of quality they want which will drive them to revisit your site again in the future and keep them coming back for the kind of content they found and you have continued to supply to them.

How To Get Other Bloggers To Send You Their Traffic For Free!

Joint Venture Partners

Joint Venture Partners are usually a company that will negotiate with you to place your page on their site or on their opt-in list and you will pay them a portion of your sales or your revenue.

The definition of a joint venture is an agreement between two or more parties to join together for the purpose of executing a particular business undertaking. The profits and losses of the enterprise are agreed to be shared between all parties. Two people, or a party of more, join together in an online joint venture to specifically do business online.

So, in plain English, an online joint venture occurs when another online business is available for you to join forces with, in order to make money. Joint ventures hold no tricks other than locating a good partner. They can also be in a wide variety of different forms.

An example of this would be a simple and rather common joint venture whereby two information marketing businesses bundle their products together in order to promote them to their combined email lists.

This type of arrangement generally has high potential. The exposure and customer base of each business is increased and both get the opportunity to make money. Each customer has the opportunity to receive benefits from the product of each business.

This is only one of a thousand possibilities with this type of joint venture. If you possess a good opt in list and someone has a great product, then their product can be promoted on your list for a percentage of the sales.

You may even be a person that is talented when it comes to marketing products and have a good idea for a product that you know your market would purchase. However, you may not have the free time or the inclination to originally create the product.

To achieve this, you could partner with a programmer or a writer to create the product. By doing this, you split the profits, as you are selling the product. As stated earlier, there are a number of options.

It has been said before that the absolute key to the success of an online joint venture is in locating the correct partner. An excellent place to find a partner is by online networking. It may be that you already work with a business that you could partner with.

Once your potential partner has been located, the first step would be to draft a proposal before you do anything else. It is necessary for you to highlight the exact thing that you would bring to the relationship and what is to be gained by your potential partner.

Here are some tips for negotiating with potential joint venture partners :

- Set up a sales letter for your site

Just like you have a sales letter for your product where you talk about the features, benefits, why your customers should buy it, etc, the same applies for joint venture partners. You've got to sell your affiliate program or joint venture opportunity – what the product is about, what benefits will they get (eg, commissions), how do they sign up, etc.

- Know your earning rates

You have to test your sales letter beforehand. Joint venture partners will want to know your stats so they know that your sales letter actually converts in the first place. Otherwise they'll just be wasting their time and resources.

- Offer a bigger commission than anyone else

You just have to do a little more than the rest of your competitors to stand out from the crowd. Usually, for digital products, the commission rate is 50%. Why not do more than what's expected and offer 75%? Or even 100%? In fact, for one ebook book launch, I offered 100% commission. Yes I gave away all my profits because I know the money is made in the backend.

- Make it easy on your partner

Don't let them do all the work, do the work for them. Give them all the ready-made tools, such as email copy (to some extent even custom-build those promo tools). Put the affiliate link in the email promos for them (instead of something like "Replace XXXX with your affiliate link").

- Leverage your results

You just need that one partner to get everything started. So leverage it by saying something like "Bob promoted it to a list of X number of people and made Y amount" or "So and so is already onboard" (creates social proof). It's the snow ball effect.

Of course, before you begin your joint venture, you first have to find a willing partner. Perhaps the easiest way is to rely on search engine giant, Google.

Start by doing a search based on your niche market keywords. Google does a great job of coming up with competitors who are focused on your same market. Along the right side of the results page Google will list its paid placement customers.

These are the companies you will want to contact. After all, they have demonstrated they have a budget for advertising and marketing since they are paying Google for placement. And since they already have this budget in place, it is quite possible they are open to utilising their capital on a Joint Venture.

Perhaps you already have someone in mind. Now it's a matter of approaching them and winning them over.

Contact information for your target partner should be easy to find. After all, it is an ecommerce website and they do not want to make it hard for their customers to contact them. You may want to start with an email message to a principal in the business, but if you can phone them, then do so, since that is a more direct route to who you want to reach.

But what should you say to attract their attention? First, you have to realise that as a business owner these people are probably inundated with people calling and asking for money or wanting help with mentoring. So that is not a good approach.

You must sell yourself to this potential joint venture partner on the basis of the fact that when you make money, so will he or she. Point out your strengths. Be prepared to back up your claims with facts, i.e., you were the number one affiliate for a particular month with one merchant. You have to show the benefit of this venture.

Just as you sell your products or services on the internet, so will you need to sell yourself and your abilities to a partner – and do so in a professional manner.

Include in your correspondence a business proposal that focuses on sales projections (profit potential, increased conversion rate, etc.) for your joint venture team. Be sure you have included all forms of contact information.

Do not get discouraged if you do not immediately get a positive response. You are going to have to be persistent, without being an annoyance. Remember that you are a salesman in this regard. Get your foot in the door and do what you can to keep it open.

A joint business venture can be just the thing you need to boost your sales even higher and realise an even greater profit. Don't be shy about promoting you and your business to another e-commerce firm. You may be amazed at where it leads.

Social Networking and Bookmarking

Social networking is one of the most quickly growing trends on the internet and has become one of the most popular ways of bookmarking and linking your sites around the internet.

Social networking sites, such as Facebook.com, Twitter.com or Myspace.com, have become such a social phenomenon that they are the most essential tools used in generating large amounts of traffic for your website or your blog page.

Social networking, like networking in real life, is done by getting your name out there and allowing it to spread.

Getting your name out there, in life and on the internet, is best done by putting it in as many places as possible.

Like a local lawn cutting business putting fliers and business cards at local restaurants, parks, telephone poles or street corners, social networking allows you to get your name out on the most populated street corners of the internet – Facebook and Twitter.

These outlets, often thought of as the realm of high schools, are being used by enormous corporations, artists and businesses to offer promotions, get the word out and drive business and sales to either their website or to their actual businesses around the world.

By using Facebook or Myspace, you can add friends and family from around the world and post your link on your page or on your wall or your status. Get friends to spread the word and add as many people as possible.

Add people you don't know and do your research to find people that may be interested in what you are doing.

Use Twitter.com to make small posts about your website. Post what will be upcoming on the page and get as many people to follow you as possible.

Use popular buzz words and try to find the right words on Twitter that people are looking for.

Using Twitter can allow you to connect to thousands of people around the web, and this method is easy to follow, easy to re-link and easy to use to find you connections that you may have never made otherwise.

Bookmarking

The below sites, among many others, allow you to submit your site to a directory of bookmarking tools and have your site entered into their search engines.

Reddit.com

Technoratie.com

Yahoo.com

Google.com

MSN.com

Del.icio.us.com

Digg.com

Newsvine.com

Bookmarksync.com

Diingo.com

Givealink.org

Groupme!.com

Readers use these sites to find popular articles on a number of different topics, and the more traffic yours gets the more likely you will be viewed by a number of people on these sites.

Submitting to Google and Yahoo will allow you to get higher ranks in their search engines and can increase the traffic to your site exponentially over a short amount of time.

Knowing the right way to use social networking and social bookmarking sites is essential and utilising all of them for one site or one article is often the most popular method.

Link each part of your page using these methods and make the chances of drawing higher traffic all the better.

Though it may take as many as 2-3 minutes to submit to one site, and as much as an hour or an hour and a half to submit to all of the sites you would like to use, it will be worth it when it comes to traffic and sales.

Myspace, Facebook and Twitter are three of the largest sites on the internet, with three of the largest user bases, and can bring you the kind of traffic you never dreamed of if utilised right.

Contest Promotions

Contest promotions are another popular way to drive traffic and earn profits on your blog page. Like other groups, webpages, companies, businesses or services, contests can excite customers and get them buying things or coming back for more.

For example, free tickets or awards at a baseball game or the Monopoly tickets offered at McDonalds restaurants – which drive the company's highest sales all year – contests might get people to purchase things that they normally would have ignored.

Contests allow readers to compete with themselves for a prize. Offering money or prizes, at amounts less than what it would have cost to generate the traffic through different methods,, will allow you to make a profit while still giving your readers a prize.

After this, you will still be left with the extra traffic that you produced because of the contest.

Giving your readers a tangible contest that they can follow is especially useful. Allow them to follow who is winning, how much time is left and what they have to do to win.

This will force them to spend as much time on your page as possible and will give you a wealth of page visits and possible advertising promotions and revenue.

To get people to take part in your contest, consider the following:

- There must be a reason for them to get involved (i.e. the prize).
- There must be a reason for them to encourage others to join, such as family, friends or other website users.

Another type of contest you can use, or promotion you can use to go along with the contest, is offering people prizes just for recruiting other people to join your site or your contest.

This kind of recruiting will not only get your readers excited about being on your page again, it will get them to get other people excited about your page as well.

Like other marketing aspects, you need to publicise your contest and for this you can use the following:

- Other relevant blogs
- Press releases
- Freebies and giveaways

In addition to offering contests and prizes on your page, you can also offer your users and readers freebies or giveaways. Much the same as using contests, freebies and giveaways will encourage your readers to visit your page as much as possible to get these freebies.

Just using the word "free" or "freebie" will trigger an emotion in some of your readers that works on most people around the world.

Getting something for nothing is an extremely strong incentive for many people, and only having to log on to your page to receive something will have people logging onto your page as much as possible to find out how to receive their freebie, find out what the freebie is and give themselves as many chances as possible to be the one to get the freebie.

Like offering prizes, offer a freebie that is nice but is less than the money you will be receiving from the extra traffic that your freebie promotion will be directing to your page.

The freebies should provide the following for your users, readers or visitors to your page:

- It should be related to your niche
- The prizes should provide value to the customer
- It should be easy to use and easy to receive

The gifts you giveaway can supplement the information on your website and can give the visitors to your website a clearer idea of your expertise and the value you are providing them.

A freebie like this will not only get people exited about visiting your page initially, it will give them reason to anticipate further freebies and get them excited to see what other pieces of information or giveaways you have to offer them on your page.

You can also use the recruiting promotion with this tactic and get extra people to visit your page.

Also, you can ask people for their contact information and use this to encourage a stronger mailing advertisement system, giving you still further exposure to your page and your product.

Tell a Friend

Tell-A-Friend Scripts are another oft-used method for generating traffic, though they may not be nearly as common as the previously mentioned methods and resources.

These scripts are promotions that can find you users and readers via web traffic redirection.

Many websites, especially websites that are selling products, do not get their big start until they have been established as a legitimate business that is offering real products at good prices and high-quality.

While large companies do not have a problem with this, you are likely not affiliated with any large companies yet and will need some way to encourage your credibility among visitors.

Telling your customers to bring a friend to your site, even if you have to give something away free, will generate more traffic. In the eyes of the "friends" who have come to your site you have more credibility as you have been recommended by someone they trust.

While the Tell-A-Friend process may be slow at first, getting enough people to tell enough friends will allow you to continue drawing in more people, and the more people and successful transactions you have, the more credibility your page and your product will have.

As your credibility goes up, you will not need to use the Tell-A-Friend promotion or script much longer; your page will be attracting customers based on its own merits.

Your page will then be trusted because it will have had so many visitors and successful transactions.

You can use this as a promotion for people visiting your site, downloading information or purchasing products.

You can give a prize for your readers telling a friend, or you can make it mandatory for people to attract another reader to the site before you give them access to certain content, allow them to purchase your products or give away a prize.

Viral Video Marketing

Viral Video Marketing has lately become one of the top ways to generate traffic to your site.

With the mixing of technologies and communication methods, and the advent of Google video and the increased popularity of YouTube and cell phone videos, video marketing has become nearly essential for those wishing to promote their page.

Viral video marketing is best done gradually and slowly and with multiple videos. Bloggers wishing to use video marketing should use multiple videos over a period of time.

Like music artists who release one song to promote their album, and allow it to disseminate the entire market and audience, video marketing is to be done the same way.

When the music artist sees the progress of their first single stagnating, they release a second single to again produce some buzz for their product or their album. The second single creates another buzz and then they release an album.

The album will be purchased because of the buzz of the first two singles.

The artists will leave the album on the market for a while by itself and then will release another single to attract the listeners who have not yet bought the album.

In this way, the music artist will try to reach as big a portion of the audience as possible by gradually releasing new material over time and maintaining a steady amount of marketing and buzz.

To encourage viral video marketing, you can publish your videos to the following very popular sites:

Metacafe.com
Yahoo! Video
Google Video
YouTube.com
Blinkx.com
Hulu.com
Veoh.com

These sites can gain a large audience because of their prominence and large number of viewers and, if your video is good enough or marketed correctly, you can reap the benefits of these resources.

For the greatest impact your video should be one or more of the following:

- funny
- unique
- interesting
- controversial

Your video should look good. If not professional, it should be organised and coherent. It should make its point clearly and give a sense that you know what you are talking about.

The video should include a link to your website that includes what is offered at your site.

Like your website, your video should give an idea of the value that you are offering, why your site is unique, what your expertise is and why your viewers or readers should visit your site over the other sites available to them in the same niche.

Follow these tips to make your video a YouTube or internet success, sensation or phenomenon (keep in mind, homemade YouTube videos have been known to generate millions of viewers in traffic):

-Keep your video short. People in the internet age have notoriously short attention spans and your video should reflect this and get to the point as quickly as possible.

- Use link baiting. Keep your video fun and cool, appeal to your audience in some way and be sure not to sound like an advertisement.

- Use proper tags. Use tags that indicate what your video is really about. Tag it with videos that will not produce much competition but will also have people looking for your video as much as possible.

- Search YouTube and find out where the traffic is. See what has a lot of views. Tag your video with something that draws a lot of views but does not have a huge amount of competition.

- Use Movie Maker to produce your video

Popular programs like Microsoft Windows and many other pieces of software offer you easy programs for making videos.

Heck, you can even use your cell phone to film videos and then easily upload them to your computer.

These videos can be short and simple, as long as the quality is not horrible and they are still making the points that they need to be making.

Make a script and pick people that are funny, good looking or appealing in front of the camera. These people will make the best impression on viewers and will have your video attracting as many people as possible.

Earning Money from Your Blog

Perhaps the most popular method of earning money for your blog, affiliate programs like ClickBank, CJ.com and other private affiliates allows you to start earning money just as soon as you can attract some advertisers.

In this method, networks like ClickBank promote products on your site and pay you up to 50% of the sales gained as a result of the advertisement on your page. You can easily create an account on ClickBank and begin searching their marketplace for different products to promote and make money from on your website.

Text Link Sales

Selling text on your page allows advertisers and other websites to advertise on your page through links or text. Popular tools include PageRank and Alexa which allow you to sell to a multitude of different sources, including forums. You can also sell links on other forums and use the service by text-link-ads.com, which automates the process of adding links and uses their own plug-in.

Private Sponsors and Banner Ads

Like the sponsors on NASCAR automobiles or on the ice of hockey rinks, sponsors can decorate your page with different sized ads. These ads can exist as small blocks on the side of your pages, as large banner ads at the top or middle of your pages, or in many other different designs.

These banners should fit in with the design and theme of your page in order to be successful. Many of the most successful blogs can charge prices as high as $10,000 for small ads that can be fit on a page 5-10 times over. The ability to capitalise profit on these opportunities is high if you can draw enough traffic.

Paid Reviews

Once your website draws enough traffic, some advertisers will pay you healthy sums to make an actual post on your blog, promoting their product. These types of paid reviews can be used by a site to gain attention for their product and can allow you to back a product that fits in with the theme of your site.

Some of the top sites for paid reviews include:

www.payperpost.com

www.blogsvertise.com

www.sponsoredreviews.com

www.reviewme.com

www.socialspark.com

Google AdSense

One of the easiest and most popular monetising methods for the inexperienced blogger is Google AdSense. This tool allows you to create an account completely free and accumulate profits with a hands-off approach.

Though there is no work to do, your blog must achieve a high level of traffic before Google AdSense will earn you any type of significant income or profit. AdSense works by placing ads of your choice on your page and paying you per click, visit or advertisement click.

With Google AdSense, blog hosters copy and paste advertising codes into the widgets on their page and the contextual ads provided by

Google affiliates appear on your website. The ads are always relevant to your webpage and use tools called the click-through rate (CTR) and cost per click (CPC) to calculate your profitability.

The CTR is derived from the positioning of the advertisement. Ads placed more strategically will draw higher traffic and earn you a higher CTR. The CPC depends on the subject of your niche and blog. Higher paying niches can earn you as much as dollars per click (such as college education and mortgages), while lower paying niches will earn you only cents (such as technology or entertainment).

While Google AdSense is the most popular pay-per-click network, others used frequently are:

Yahoo! Publisher Network (YPN)

BidVertiser

Chitika

Clicksor

CPM Networks

Slightly different that CPC networks, cost per mille (CPM) advertising networks pay you not for clicks on your advertisement, but for views to your page, which can be a great tool for blogs that are generating a lot of traffic, but not a lot of advertisement clicks.

CPM networks pay a certain amount for every 1,000 visits to your page and can vary from under $1 to many dollars. A page with a CPM of $1 will earn this amount for 1,000 views and, for a page that can draw many thousands per day, this can slowly add up.

Like CPC networks, CPM rates also vary with the position of the ad and the format of the ad on the page. With better networks, the CPM rate will increase. Advertisements at the top of the page will naturally draw a higher CPM than advertisements used at the bottom of the page or on the borders. CPMs can vary between $0.10 and $10 and can come in many different shapes, sizes, formats, layouts and pixels, all of which will effect your total CPM amount.

The most frequently used CPM networks include:

Casale Media
Value Click
Advertising.com
Right Media
Tribal Fusion
Burst Media

Direct Banner Advertising

The most profitable and perhaps most difficult way of generating advertising profits for your blog page is by selling your own advertising space. Selling your own space will allow you to earn the money that is usually lost through advertising hosting sites and affiliate sites – essentially, you are cutting out the middle man.

Formats include the 125 x 125 button ad, the 300 x 250 rectangle ad, the 120 x 600 skyscraper ad and the 728 x 90 leaderboard ad. These ads and this kind of advertising require that you have a large blog audience to begin with and force you to handle the managing process yourself, whereas programs like Google AdSense are completely hands-off.

Kontera

Kontera is a tool that advertises based on the specific words used in your blog posts. One of the newest methods of monetising your blog, Kontera has become popular in the past year as a way of bringing money to past and future posts, not just current ones.

A newly growing source, Kontera is expected to grow in importance in the following years and offers users a way of reaping large profits when used correctly.

Called text-link ads, words in the content of your blog can be clicked on to access affiliates sites.

Other resources include:

TNX
LinkWorth
Text-Link-Brokers
Text-Link-Ads
DigitalPoint Link Sales Forum

Affiliate Marketing

A widely used practice across the entire internet, affiliate marketing can allow blog hosters to earn a commission by selling affiliate (other people's) products to the traffic generated on a blog.

Some affiliates will pay based on sales generated from your page and other affiliates will pay based on the cost per action (CPA) or the cost per lead (CPL).

Affiliates combine the other methods of advertising, but pay in this commission model. Affiliates can use banner ads, text links or any other kind of ad and can be found in different affiliate programs or through publishers like Dreamhost or SEOBook.

Some of the other popular affiliate networks include:

ClickBank
Azoogle Ads
Link Share
Commission Junction

Monetisation Widgets

Widgets have lately become an extremely popular tool on the internet for many different things and chief among them is monetising and earning profit from your blog. Popular monetising widget sources are SmartLinks and Widgetbucks. These services usually run pay per click systems, though many also use text ads, and can employ affiliate advertising in some situations.

While they are not traditionally the same as any of the other tools or methods, they are similar. The chief difference among them is that widgets make it easier to add the ads to your website.

Top widget tools include:

WidgetBucks

SmartLinks

ScratchBack

Sponsored Reviews

The pioneer in the sponsored review model was PayPerPost, who emerged as a way to pay bloggers to write a post about a certain subject. Other popular sponsored review sites have emerged since, including ReviewMe and Sponsored Reviews, and have improved and altered the process to a point of near perfection.

Writing sponsored reviews will allow a blogger to write about a specific person, product, service or site and often pay well compared with other types of advertising on blogs.

Some bloggers veer away from sponsored reviews because they provide a way to blemish editorial credibility, though in some cases a blogger will run into a review that they agree with and it will allow the blogger to earn money by adding what could be seen as normal content.

Sponsored review networks:

Sponsored Reviews

Review Me

PayPerPost

Smorty

BlogVertise

RSS Feed Ads

RSS has quickly emerged as one of the top internet marketing and dissemination tools. It has given owners a way to attract readers and monetise their pages like never before.

Firstly what does RSS stand for or mean?

RSS stands for different things. RSS is a way of showing content (news, pictures, mp3s) without having to go to different web addresses to get it. Say you want to read the news at CNN, foxnews and read some comics. Normally you would go to the sites and have all the ads and junk pop-up, but you just want the news! Enter RSS. Using programs known as "aggregators", you can see many "feeds" at the same time.

Resources like Feedburner have given publishers the ability to sign-up and start showing off their CPM based advertising information.

Finally, some blogs are also opting to sell banners or sponsored messages on their feed directly. John Chow and Marketing Pilgrim are two examples.

Related links:

Feedburner
BidVertiser
Pheedo

Single Column or Event Sponsors

Single column or event sponsors work much like the sponsored segments on different live television shows. Like a certain recurring segment on

SportsCenter, single column sponsors offer money to have their name associated with a "column" on your webpage. These columns can include surveys, interviews, reviews, podcasts or videos.

Increasing the monetisation for a website, this method allows users to gain advertising for just one segment of their page, while still reaping the profits of the rest of the page separately. Affiliates are able to seek out opportunities on different pages and find a "column" that will appeal directly to a certain, and usually obvious, audience or segment of a site's audience.

Premium Content

Another popular way to monetise your blog, that often has absolutely nothing to do with the advertising methods illustrated in the other sections, is by hosting premium content.

This ability to host "premium" content will allow bloggers to give away much of the content of their blog for free, while charging for the more exclusive sections of their page.

This method allows popular sites with many subscribers to earn large profits from the advertising hosted on their free pages, on top of the membership fees used to pay for premium content.

Private Forums

Forums on the internet have become an exclusively popular way of hosting movies, music, sports and niche topics and sites. While public forums are extremely popular and accessed freely, private forums can charge one-time or monthly fees to earn profits from users willing to pay these fees to access a forum.

Private forums charging fees obviously need to have built up a level of credibility and importance and need to provide their subscribing members with quality content that is of real value to the user.

Popular software used to create forum pages include:

Simple Machines forum
phpBB
vBulletin
Vanilla

Job Boards

Job boards have recently become a popular tool used to supplement profits and traffic to a site. In order to add a job board, a site needs to be aimed at a very focused niche and have built itself up to a certain level of success.

Once you have achieved the traffic and credibility, you can charge from $10 to $100 for job listing on your site.

Some of the popular software used for job boards includes:

Jobbex
SimplyHired Job-o-matic
Web Scribe Job Board
JobThread

Marketplaces

Among the most difficult ways of monetising your blog is turning it into an online marketplace. This method requires quite a bit of planning and internal organisation and forces a user to maintain a level of organisation that may take much more time than running the actual blog.

With a marketplace, site hosters can allow users to buy, trade and sell products on their site and charge a small processing fee for each transaction. These sites allow like-minded people to meet each other and provide outlets and sources for products.

While this method could turn into large profits with success, the need to outsource work would almost always be necessary to find a coder to produce the tools on your site.

Paid Surveys and Polls

Among the more interesting tools for monetising your blog are paid surveys. These services pay you revenue to run small surveys and polls on your website about their product or their service.

Selling or Renting Internal Pages

Since nearly the beginning of monetisation on the internet, selling or renting internal pages has allowed bloggers to rent particular pages on their site to buyers or advertisers looking to host content to a wide audience.

Highlighter Posts from Sponsors

Another idea that was popularised initially by one company (in this case, Techmeme), highlighting posts from sponsors is a tool that lets bloggers and site hosters show off editorial posts on a column.

In these editorial posts, often relegated to the side columns of the page, buyers of advertising space can post whatever they like in a space that is often left for sites with very significant traffic.

Pop-ups and Pop-unders

A frustration to many site-goers and readers, pop-ups and pop-unders can be an especially effective way of advertising for many websites.

Pop-ups and pop-unders, doing exactly what their names implies, are generally looked at as spam by many users, but can be an effective way of advertising for companies and finding goods and services for readers and visitors.

Pop-up blockers have become one main hinderance to pop-up and pop-under advertising, and have allowed many internet browsers to avoid the annoyance of pop-ups and hence not many of these paid opportunities last as long as they might otherwise.

Popular networks that use pop-up ads are:

Tribal Fusion
Adversal
PopupAd
PayPopup

Audio Ads

Called Pay Per Play (or PPP) ads by many people, audio ads are a type of advertising that was first introduced by Net Audio Ads. A simple concept that works exactly as it sounds audio ads are used every time a visitor enters the page.

Once an internet users clicks onto your page, a short (perhaps five second) audio clip will play on your page. Because the clip is short and played from the advertisement, the visitor will likely not be able to stop the advertisement, providing for a 100% viewing rate.

This high rate allows bloggers to receive a very high CPM rate, often as high as $5.

Selling Your Website

Trading and flipping websites is also a popular way of making money. A last choice when it comes to monetising your blogs, selling your site can allow you to earn a nice lump sum of money. Selling your blog may provide a once-off high payout, but it also may also deprive you of the opportunity to generate income over time.

DigitalPoint and Sitepoint are two forums that connect site owners to buyers, and selling a website can earn an owner as much as many dozen times the monthly revenues.

Selling an EBook

A monetising method that has stood the test of time, selling eBooks based on your web content will allow you to efficiently generate revenue for your site, independent of your site and in addition to your site.

It will promote traffic and promote further expertise and will give you the opportunity to further hire freelance writers to make a larger splash on your website and your niche network.

Selling a Hardcover Book

Your website can be the platform to make money using other methods. With your website or blog you can promote another products and one of the most popular products is the hardcover book.

> *"Promoting your own book on your site can afford you a very large profit..."*

Selling their physical book through their website is a route many authors and journalist travel. Promoting your own book on your site can afford you a very large profit if done successfully.

Gaining authority, success, fans and notoriety on your blog before later publishing a book is a popular process. By accumulating a large enough audience and proving your knowledge with years of experience on your website, you can find yourself a large audience for a book that may boost your earning exponentially.

Following is a list of publishers and publishing services:
www.TheGlobalPublishingGroup.com
www.HowToWriteABestSeller.com
iUniverse
WordClay
Lulu

Selling Templates or WordPress Themes

Themes can be added to your blog on websites like WordPress, and sold, to make you money and personalise your site further. These themes can serve as templates and links to your site that other people could use to host their own sites or homepages.

Offering Consulting and Related Services

Offering your services based on your blog, your site, or your niche is one way to make money. These services can be given through the internet or outside of the internet and can be based on your expertise displayed on your website.

If your customers trust you enough and value your knowledge to a high enough degree, they may be willing to pay you to consult for them or advise them. Because the information you would be providing them with is much more personal and time consuming, you could use this to charge a much higher fee, such as a large hourly rate, to provide your services for clients.

Creating an Email List or Newsletter

Creating newsletters or e-mailing subscriptions is another way to spread the word about your site or your niche. E-mail lists and newsletters are a popular way to disseminate information from people to their family and friends and associates without getting them to actually visit your site.

Yaro Starak, a popular, well-paid, and well known internet marketer, has used e-mailing lists to build a blog that is one of the most profitable on the internet and makes him many thousands of dollars every month.

Below is a list of software to manage email newsletters:

AWeber

SendStudio NX

PHP Autoresponder

Constant Contact

Mentoring Programs

Turning your blog or website into a mentoring program allows you to attract visitors who are looking for an educational and enriching experience.

These sites teach and give knowledge to their visitors and audience, and educating this audience is among the biggest and most profitable industries on the internet.

Creating a mentoring program for your website, one that is related to your niche, will allow you to squeeze a profit from a correctly coordinated program. These programs intertwine different forms of media to create a range of information and lessons that are both interesting and informational for the user.

Creating a Conference Around Your Website/Niche

Creating a conference around your particular website or niche can allow you to draw in thousands of dollars outside of normal advertising income earned through the everyday running of your website or blog.

If your website gains enough followers, enough credibility and enough power, and becomes a leading authority in your particular niche, you may be able to host events outside of the internet – off in the real world.

Hosting conference around your website can allow you to tap into a totally new stream of revenue and can allow you to earn real money in real ways and at real events.

E-mail Marketing

Another top method of marketing your blog or webpage, e-mail marketing will allow you to squeeze the most out of your site even when people are not visiting your site.

Like sending fliers or advertisements in the postal mail, e-mail marketing allows you to reach users that may have never heard of your page.

By using e-mail marketing, you can alert readers or potential readers of what is going on with your site, why they should visit your site and it can tease them with some of the value and important information that you are providing on your site.

With e-mail marketing you can send people the following:

- small lessons that illustrate what can be found on your page
- updates to your site
- new information posted recently
- products for sale
- services
- special promotions, prizes, contests or giveaways

- special content not seen on the site
- short instructional guides
- press releases
- links to videos

Any of these forms of content can be used in your e-mail marketing campaign and you can even copy and paste small blurbs of content directly from your site to make the e-mail marketing campaign more cost effective.

You can have your users give their e-mail addresses upon sign up and send them periodic e-mail updates.

You can also gather e-mail address through other sources and send your e-mail marketing materials to people who have not yet signed up for your site.

You can outsource the e-mail marketing to freelance writers to spruce up the content that you could be sending out to possibly thousands of people.

Your e-mail marketing letters should be between 200 and 700 words and should clearly state what your site is about and what you are trying to do.

Like articles on your actual site, use a catchy headline and write about a popular topic. Use short sentences and short paragraphs, and compose your e-mail with an introduction, a body and a closing.

Your e-mail campaign should provide some value, but should not make the content on your website irrelevant.

It should encourage people to use the content in your e-mail, and then go to your site for further value and information.

E-mail marketing can make or break your blog or niche website and that is why it has become so important to many and so widely used.

> *To Fast Track Your Success Model Yourself on other High Achievers.*

Darren J Stephens

International Bestselling Author & Speaker

CHAPTER 5

The eBay
Phenomenon

Chapter 5
The eBay Phenomenon

With the Internet, starting a business from scratch can be done easier than it has ever been done. Internet businesses often require little to no start up cost and can be completed – and made profitable – by just about anyone with the desire, know-how and determination to get the thing off the ground and running.

There are hundreds of examples of people who have made money on the Internet and have used their personal resources to transition a small start up into a minor fortune – and all within a small timeframe. Some have done it part time in as little as 24 months, while others have done it even more quickly, and many others in hardly longer than those two years.

Whatever walk of life you are in, there are options online that can take you to the kind of money that you have always dreamed of and this can be done with less than full time attention.

One popular market for making money on the Internet is none other than the largest marketplace and auction site online; eBay. eBay is a phenomenon around the world and the means to making money through this outlet has been well documented by many people – including, most notably, Matt and Amanda Clarkson of BiddingBuzz.com.

Matt and Amanda Clarkson are two everyday people that went from zero to millions in just two years and they have eBay to thank for this. Their website, www.biddingbuzz.com, is a hotbed of tips and a treasure chest of information and can set you on the path to doing the same – all through the simple process of buying and selling.

Matt and Amanda Clarkson were a carpenter and a personal trainer, respectively, and they now use the simple auction website of eBay to make over $50,000 every month in their personal business. With tips like the ones on biddingbuzz.com, they were able to make this kind of money all the while working only about 10 hours per week. They were able to put their profits on auto-pilot and were able to emerge with a lucrative earning machine.

They had had enough of their daily struggle and, within three years, they had developed one of Australia's most successful eBay business and a comfort in their professional lives that they had never known. Within eight months there were making $50,000 every month and were able to automate about 90 percent of the process, drastically cutting down the time they had to put into the business on a regular basis.

Today, while they still run their eBay business, they travel the world speaking about this subject and sharing the secrets to be had at their website; BiddingBuzz.com.

Making money on eBay does indeed require skill, but it is something that can be learned by anyone with the passion to do so, and can make you a millionaire in a few short years. Buying or selling on this marketplace will give you access to millions of people around the world and the opportunity for transactions is ever-present on a site like eBay.

Even if you have never sold a thing on eBay – never signed up to the site or purchased anything from it – you can start up your business in less than a day and be on your way to making money in nearly no time. With a proven system, you can make as much as $50,000 a year, all while working just ten hours every week, or a few short hours every day, like BiddingBuzz.com founder Matt and Amanda Clarkson.

It may sound too be good to be true, but the formula has been used around the world and can propel you into a different economic bracket in a short time. A home based eBay business can be started from your computer room, even if you have seemingly no idea what you are doing, and you can move away from the minutiae of your 9-5, and into the lap of luxury that you have always sought.

If you would like to make yourself financially secure in your later years, simply following this formula – this "wealth vehicle" – to your riches. Begin your journey in the rat race, and find yourself enjoying business from your computer chair in a few short years.

It is no secret or fluke that some make money in this kind of "work." This line of financial stability is enjoyed by about 1.3 million people around the world, and they use the website to sell different physical items across the globe.

And it is not just the number of people working this way that adds to the legitimacy of eBay, but also the overwhelming number of members and transactions that take place each day on the auction site.

> **"...over $1 billion spent on eBay every week..."**

There are more than 5 million members on eBay each day that spend in excess of $141 million each day on different products. This equals a total of over $1 billion spent on eBay every week of the year.

The influence of this site is worldwide and the scope of your ability to reap the rewards of eBay can be hard to understand at first. The profits are out there, however, and all it takes is patience, determination and the will to make it work. You can make a small fortune selling things you may never have dreamed of and you can remove yourself from the monotony of coffee and commutes and into the upper echelon of comfort and happiness.

As with many other aspects of the Internet, there is no better time to reap the rewards of this resource than now. Matt and Amanda Clarkson realised that eBay is growing at the same rapid rate as the rest of the online world, and there over 250 million eBay members registered. This number of people, if fit into one country, would make it the fifth largest nation in the world. So you are, in essence, opening yourself to a buying market the size of a worldwide superpower nation.

If you own your own business, you can sell old or surplus materials and might find yourself making more through these sales than you do in your normal business, or it could be a very comfortable secondary income.

Many eBay users, however, are using the auction site in a way that is far less than efficient. They are losing money on sales as they are posting items and hoping for the best. These users are not running their business in a smart way and are simply failing because of their lack of knowledge or lack of effort.

To those in the know there are a few keys ways to make a fortune on eBay. Here are five of the most popular ways to make this money:

1. eBay Hobbyist

As an eBay hobbyist, you can sell items for fun and create an extra stream of income on the side. This can be used as a supplement to your main income and will give you the chance to have extra bill or spending money. This method is perfect for those with a comfortable job who are looking for extra cash. If you are looking to make a few extra dollars, or reap in thousands like Matt and Amanda Clarkson, you can follow the tips outlined here and on BiddingBuzz.com.

As an eBay hobbyist, you can sell junk from your house or your friends' houses, or you can find an endless supply of things at shopping outlets, opportunity shops, Salvation Army stores and used stores. Flea markets and garage sales are also popular places for hobbyists to find their products to sell. You can earn as much as $1000 every week just selling many dozens of these types of items.

One downside is that this may be among the most time consuming of ways to sell on eBay, because you will not be able to automate the sales. With this method, you will have a lot of "one-off" sales, and you will have to keep posting new items as you find them.

2. Drop Shipping

The next method of eBay selling, drop-shipping, is another popular way to start out an eBay business if you are new to the craft or the practice. This kind of selling allows you to earn money if you are on a tight budget and lets you make money while you are working from your laptop, wherever you are in the world.

This is among the most common ways of getting your feet wet on eBay and will allow you to move onto more automated, easier and more profitable ventures on the auction site.

Drop shipping means that you will be dealing with wholesalers. These wholesalers will be handling the shipping for you, and you will not have to handle any of the stock yourself.

Using photos supplied from the wholesaler, you will sell the product they have to offer. Once you have collected the money from the buyer, you pay the wholesaler and they then ship the item out to the buyer. The difference between what your buyer pays you and what you pay the wholesaler is your profit.

The process can be completed without any expenses on your part (apart from eBay fees) and is probably the simplest type of eBay selling.

Disadvantages can be found in the fact that you are not doing all of the work yourself and are therefore relying on the wholesalers to get the items to the consumer on time and consistently. Another disadvantage is that you have no control over the stock, which means you have no ability to ensure that your wholesaler always has sufficient quantity of product to fill all your orders.

The last disadvantage can perhaps be the largest, but you can defeat this problem by focusing on selling a large quantity of products. With drop shipping, because the wholesalers are doing the largest portion of the work, your profits will be low, and will only average 5% to 25% of the actual selling price. But, as we said, if you focus on selling a large quantity of items, 5-25% profit from the selling price is still a good amount of money.

3. Consignment Business

This method of selling allows you to sell another person's goods. It is another popular way for eBay beginners to make money and can produce a higher level of profits than the type of selling done with drop-shipping. With consignment selling, you agree to sell another person's items for them. In exchange for you using your time, knowledge and skills on eBay to sell these items, you receive a percentage of the sale price, after eBay fees have been deducted. You determine the profit which you will receive in agreement with the person whose items you are selling. This can be as much as 50% of the sale price after eBay fees have been paid; you will have to decide what is the most fair.

Chances are, if you are effective and efficient, you will be able to earn larger profits either because your services are so valuable, or because you are selling a very high quantity of items.

You can supply yourself with a never ending list of products if you handle your consignment business the correct way. You can do this through advertisements and agreements, and approaching store owners and individuals with the offer to sell their products for them. If you have the ability to find products, like Matt and Amanda Clarkson, you can end up making millions. For more tips on how to run a successful consignment business, head to biddingbuzz.com.

Knowing how to approach people and what to say is important, and once people know how talented you are at selling, they will be more and more willing to leave their products with you to sell. At the beginning you will find it hard to say no, refusing to turn down even the smallest profit. But in the end, you will find yourself forced to say no as you will not be able to take in all of the business that you are attracting.

4. eBay Arbitrage

This method of selling means you buy low and sell high, making money on eBay and allowing you to take advantage of the poor selling practices of other eBay users. You will be able to make part time or full time income streams by reselling items from those who have listed them wrong, who did not make the full profit they should have, or who have listed them at the wrong time or with the incorrect specifications.

5. Sell Your Own Products

This can be the easiest method for those already running a personal, home or small business, and selling your own products will allow you to capitalise on your own personal hobbies and passions. There are countless people doing the same, and this will give you the chance to stay tuned in to an industry that you are obviously already well-versed in.

If you own a product or a business, chances are you are already mass producing your product and making a profit off of it in your normal business procedures. With this added benefit of selling on eBay, you will be able to reap nearly full profits by selling additional products to people around the world.

You will be able to automate the selling of these products as you become good at it and you will be seeing larger profits than you ever expected.

The beauty of this kind of selling is that your products do not need to be high tech, expensive to make or difficult to get. You can simply sell your expertise in a product like a book or a DVD, which will be very low cost to make, and you can make a large profit off of it with a high price tag. If your product is a good one, people will be willing to pay high amounts for your expertise and advice.

With the fewest downsides of any form of eBay selling, using your own products can be a very lucrative business endeavor and is just one of many, many ways to make good money selling on eBay. The easy part is finding items to sell on eBay. The difficult part comes when you decide to take the time and action to actually create something of value through your eBay selling.

This will take both action and thinking, and the planning and strategy involved in this concept can be time spent that will make you many thousands of dollars. There are 12 main steps that you can use to achieve your success on eBay and these are detailed for you in the following paragraphs.

Step 1 – Plan for your success

Planning is an essential part of any business endeavor and selling on eBay is no different. You have to open your mind and expect to be successful and this will allow you to take advantage of the opportunities presented to you.

Step 2 – Record your ideas

Another essential activity for money-making, business and online endeavors, you have to be able to come up with new ideas and track these ideas. You have to open your mind and track all of the opportunities that you come up with. You need to find programs that tell you what is selling, where it is selling and when it is selling – even what time of the day is the best to list products.

You need to know how much profit is possible and take all of the guessing work out of your money-making. It is through these devices that you will be able to give people exactly what they are looking for. Like Matt and Amanda Clarkson, you need to understand exactly what people are looking for. You need to do this research before establishing an eBay business you can put on auto-pilot, and your first step is with a resource like Biddingbuzz.com.

Step 3 – Get started today and keep practicing

As the saying goes, there is no time like the present, and this is especially true in the case of the Internet and eBay. Like anything you wish to excel in, you should start right away and develop yourself through practice, practice and practice.

You need to know what works best, why people attract higher bids and why people are listing higher in search results. You need to learn the steps to automating your business and you need to know how to put the least work in for the most money in return. These can only be learned through research and practice.

Step 4 – Find the hottest markets

As with any job search, any product selling campaign and any money making scheme, you need to know what is working and what is selling. You need to look for markets that are largely untapped and you need to get into the minds of customers and consumers. You need to know the most about your market and find out how to make money from what consumers want.

Step 5 – Plan for long term profits

As you would with any business venture, you need to plan long term for your eBay business. You need to put yourself into a position to make a fast buck now and continue making that buck well into the future; plan to make an asset out of your business. You need to know how to complete the steps that will keep the process running for your children well into the future.

You should take the emotion out of your business. Do not become attached to the product; become attached instead to the selling.

Decide on the outcome of your business. Decide how much you want to make and what you want your eBay business to look like and then put the steps in place to work towards that outcome.

Step 6 – Sourcing products

You can find products to sell that you have at home or you can source products from your work, local businesses or drop-shippers. You can go to wholesalers, try arbitrage, or go to trade shows and import your own products from all over.

Step 7 – Create the best listings on eBay

Like any other product that is sold, in some respects, it is all about the presentation. When you are selling on eBay, you need to promote your product well and this comes from having a good listing. If your listing is better than all of your competition, there is a good chance you will get both more views and more sales.

You should describe your product accurately and in detail and, if you can, create a story around your product, to relate to your buyer and let them know you understand their problems and trials and what they want from your product. You should also use a plethora of pictures, so people know exactly the quality that they are buying, and you should point out all of the key features and benefits.

Use all of these tactics to make your buyers comfortable buying from you and provide them with little opportunity to have any doubts about the product. Maximise your profits by making the best listings that you can and you will position yourself to sell more items that you have ever dreamed and much more than even your top competitors in the same niche.

Step 9 – Use the correct listing format

You should know the difference between the different listing formats and use these to let your buyers know exactly what they will be getting from your sale. An auction format is used for customers to bid on your items until a set time. A fixed price is where customers can pay a certain amount to buy your product right away. Listing them in your eBay store allows you to control your sale from your own mini-website within eBay, and using the classified ads gives you the chance to advertise your services and sell them to the highest bidder.

Step 9 – Customer service

Essential to organisations, stores, companies and services around the world, customer service is important in every aspect of business. Many eBay sellers ignore this, and bad customer service can distract, frustrate and discourage buyers. You want to create and cultivate relationships with customers that are pleased with your service and then they will be happy to come back to you time after time. In the early days, biddingbuzz.com's Matt and Amanda Clarkson were able to provide their own high level of customer service. But they were soon able to expand this to an automated service that made their work all that much easier.

You have to portray a positive customer service experience without ever meeting or speaking with you customers. You have to do this through your listings, your pages and your correspondence. If a customer has reservations about your service, if they are not catered to adequately or quickly enough, they may be inclined to seek out another seller with whom to do business.

Many sellers believe the transaction is over once the purchase is made and the money is sent, but this is simply not the case. The transaction should not be considered completed until the customer is happy and willing to refer people to you. The perfect time to cultivate this relationship is by following up with a customer and making them feel comfortable with a sale as soon as the transaction has been made, and even into the future.

Step 10 – Dominate your specific category

You need to dominate your category to be a top seller on eBay, and this can only by done by implementing the correct steps to make your business the best that it can be. You may not know how to do this in the beginning, but you will learn that it is not such an overwhelming process. You need to know how to become any expert in any niche and dominate the competition. You also need to know how to compel the bidders to understand that you have the best product, and then you need to repeat these steps in several categories – as well as related niches – to give yourself the bets chance at the highest profits.

Step 11 – Automate your business

The most exciting and potentially most profitable step on this list, automating your business will give you the opportunity to put the money-making on auto-pilot, and coast into the kind of money that you know you should be making.

The automation process is why this business idea is so attractive in the first place and the daily processes that can be automated allow us more free time to do the things that we love. It allows us the freedom to only have to work 10 hours a week at making all of that money.

The following things can be automated to save you time:

- The listing process
- Customer payment reminders
- Feedback from customers
- Invoicing and payments
- Banking

Doing these things, as well as the preceding steps, will put you in the best position to glide through the process. You must first put in the time and work to realise your eBay business. Once this is done you will be able to make all of your money with as little as one or two hours on your computer each day.

Like Matt and Amanda Clarkson, you too can reach the kind of profit that you have dreamed about and always wanted. Using the practices and techniques of the Clarkson's, and the ones found on BiddingBuzz. com, you can turn this eBay dream into a reality, and be counting your dollars in your spare time every week.

" *Entrepreneurs are visionaries – they see things other people don't see.* **"**

Dame Anita Roddick

Founder of the Body Shop

CHAPTER 6

Making a Million Dollars
from Membership Sites

Chapter 6
Making a Million Dollars from Membership Sites

Membership sites are quickly evolving into the way of the future and have become one of the most essential ways for experts in each niche to increase their profits as people fight to find the best information and the leading experts.

Membership sites allow you to make money from your skills, knowledge and expertise, and allow you to connect users to what they are looking for – all at different price scales and greatly varying pay rates. Under this system, you get paid for the higher level information and reap rewards from the specialised services in which you are an expert.

Levels of Membership

With different levels of membership, you offer your clients a choice. The choice can be in the features on your website, or you can give them more intimate access to you, your associates and your products.

You can charge as little as $10 per month for membership to your lowest programs or you can charge as much as thousands of dollars every year for your highest programs. The higher programs can include group phone calls and personal attention, while the lower grades might include only access to your website.

With the lowest level of membership, you are simply guaranteeing that there is some commitment from the client. With increasing levels of commitment, people become more and more dependent on your services and are willing to pay increasing prices for this. It helps to provide multiple payment options and to give discounts for engaging in longer membership periods, such as yearly membership.

The next level of membership can be a yearly program. This can include monthly calls, email campaign, training sessions or audio recordings and can be offered in simple formats like CDs or digital MP3s. This kind of interaction can be delegated to someone working for you and will allow you to save your time for the higher paying membership clients.

With the next level of membership, you can charge considerably more. If this is the case, and you are running a planning or coaching program, you can offer both personal help and help from your master coaches in your absence. There will not be the benefits of the highest level, but you can still host live events, and make them exclusive to members of this rank.

The top-level membership can be very highly priced, and can be limited to a small amount of people. It can be the short list of people who have direct access to your skills anytime they want them and they will also enjoy all of the benefits of the other membership levels. You can offer private retreats and make people sign up for the higher levels of membership through an exclusive application process.

These higher levels of membership will be what drives your business and should involve increased contact with you, the main professional and expert. The fees should increase exponentially and as the amount of work done by you goes up, so too will the rewards.

The application form for the higher levels will allow you to make sure that the people entering the program have the appropriate level of skill and the appropriate level of interest in the subject. It will allow you to network with other members of the group and stay tuned in to what is needed in the field at the time. It will also serve to put a sought-after barrier of entry into the top membership level, and that will make the fight for these positions all the more competitive and rewarding.

You should make the highest levels sign up for longer periods of time, such as a full year at a time, and provide larger discounts for the longer periods of membership. There should be options, and these should reflect the choices for different people, different skills and different dollar amounts.

These membership plans will allow your clients to sign up for your site at a level that they are comfortable with and it will allow them to relate with your at their own level – depending on their comfort with you, how much access they would like and how much they are willing to spend. It is essential for them to have choices and it is also important for them to be comfortable with knowing what they will get out of their choices.

These plans also set ground rules for how much people will be getting and, if the service is good, they will always clamor for more – more services, more often, more features, more extras and more quality. This will mean more money, more profit, more freedom and more members.

You also need to be sure not to shun the people in lower level memberships in place of the higher members. The lower levels are also essential for your business, as they make up the largest percentage of your memberships, and are the ones networking with other future members. These will also be the people that will eventually move up to your higher membership levels.

Multiple Membership Areas

Instead of making some areas accessible to some members, you can create multiple sites within one model. Depending on the software that you are using, this can be done to allow the different levels of membership access to different programs on your website.

Save your best ideas, design and content for the higher membership levels, and use these to emphasise to your clients that they are indeed moving up – moving up in their membership status, moving up in the world and moving up in their ability to take from your knowledge, skill and expertise.

Every time a member purchases a higher membership level, you could open a new portion of your site, allowing them to explore information that was never available to them before.

Having one site will allow you to more easily automate the process, control your clients and keep them ultimately organised and efficient. You could edit and organise the site as one, knowing that only some members will have access to the portions you are changing. With these changes, you will not have to worry about some content that will not apply to others. You can focus simply on making the content specialised for each group.

Membership sites are a business model within themselves; however, it is possible to make a membership site that complements an existing business. The membership site can become another stream of income into your business, either as an additional offering to your current customers or through attracting new customers that you may not currently be reaching.

If you are setting up a membership site for your business, you could give access to the site only to people who have enrolled in a particular service or who have purchased a specific product. With these abilities, you will be able to give them access to certain expertise and even profit from it. You will be able to reward their loyalty, and give them further reason to seek out your assistance.

Like a frequent flyer program, having a membership site for your business will give your members the freedom to track their importance within your business and will give them perks that others will not have access to.

It can be the focal point of your client's experience with your company and these kinds of sites will give them the opportunity to reach out to you on a level that they are comfortable with, and one that promotes both client loyalty and company loyalty.

Unsubscribing

Unsubscribing may be an option for all of your members and clients at one point and this can happen for any number of reasons. If and when your clients are looking to unsubscribe, this should be a simple process that is comfortable for them to complete.

It should not be made so easy, that they can easily rid themselves of your services with a few clicks, but you should not go out of your way to make it a hassle for them. When people are trying to unsubscribe, it may be because they have noticed charges on their bills lately and have realised that they are not taking advantage of your services enough to justify the prices that they are paying for them.

If this is the case, and they are hassled through phone calls and email to unsubscribe, this will leave a bad taste in their mouths. This will hurt the brand of your company, the viral and buzz marketing that takes places by word of mouth, and may hurt you in the long run. While you certainly do not want to lose members, you should not make it impossible for them to find their way out when necessary.

You could also create a program where members sign up for certain portions of a course and the payments will stop as soon as they want them to stop or as soon as the course is over. Clients will feel comfortable in knowing that they will not be signed up for years at a time, or that they can opt out of the course if necessary. As with other plans, though, you should make sure to offer the largest discounts for the longer a client signs up.

> *"...offer the largest discounts for the longer a client signs up."*

You can provide incentives to sign up for the higher levels of membership and you should make sure that all of your clients know that sticking around will give them the best benefits. If they are considering leaving after one section of the program, let them know that they will be missing out on important steps present in the next part of the program.

Keeping Your Clients

In addition to attracting clients and getting them to sign up, it is also essential for you to keep your clients as long as possible as, in general, it is less expensive to keep an existing client than it is to get a new one.

You need to keep them engaged in their membership and keep them focused on the things that they are trying to accomplish.

You should make it a point to encourage your clients to use their membership areas, to communicate with you and to get the most out of the membership as is possible. You should let them know that there is a support system and that you are there to answer their questions and to add as much value for them as possible. They should feel comfortable that the system is not on auto-pilot and it is in their best interests to stay engaged in their membership as long as possible.

Encouraging Participation

To keep people committed, invested and involved, encourage them to participate in their membership as much as possible. You can do this in a number of diverse ways. One popular way of encouraging participation is through forums. Give your members the ability to interact with other members, post their opinions, learn as much as possible and stay as involved as possible. A forum is an active part of a website and offering these kinds of things will keep people as involved as they have ever been.

The difficult part will be filling an empty forum at the beginning. You can encourage people to start using a forum, but you can start the process yourself, or with an employee or a small group of clients (as small as even one). Once you get some activity going, encourage people to visit everyday, or even a few times a week.

This will start a dialogue that will ultimately propel into something worthwhile that will keep people coming to your site time after time. It can produce a feeling of community and it can set your website up for the kinds of interactions that will keep people interested for years.

When you have membership sites, you will be able to constantly send relevant and helpful content to your clients. This kind of content can keep them interested and can be an extra perk of their memberships.

Reminders via email will allow you to give them more interesting and original content. You can also give them access to DVDs, training manuals and webinars that will keep them interested as much as ever.

When you send out emails, people are more likely to communicate with you and seek out your services. This can be one of your most important methods for picking up new clients, getting new business and adding onto your customer base.

Clients will be spending more time with you if there is an open line of communication and staying close to your clients will lead to a stronger sense of community and a likely increase in memberships and membership lengths.

Letting your members know how appreciated they are will give you the opportunity to keep them longer and retain their interest longer than ever.

> *The Internet is changing everything, and has changed the world in such a short period of time, and will continue to change things in very positive ways that we have yet to anticipate.*

Pierre Omidyar
Founder of eBay

CHAPTER 7

Building Your Internet
Millionaire eBusiness

Chapter 7
Building Your Internet Millionaire eBusiness

There are a number of other things you can do with your website to help you continue to build your Internet millionaire eBusiness. These methods will let you take advantage of strategies that allow you to enhance your name by getting the word out and by continuing to give customers and followers what they are looking for.

Linking with Other Pages

Linking with other webpages can be another indispensable tool that will allow you to achieve the kind of results that you are looking for. By linking to other pages, and allowing other pages to link to you, you can create a mutually beneficial relationship with other webpages and businesses.

For example, if you are selling old relics and items, you could link to someone who is an artist selling paintings of the period. Because people looking at your page may also be interested in the art, and vice versa, this will allow you to gain views from the other page, and allow the other page to in turn gain views from your page.

You can link to any related or non-related site, and agree with the other page to promote each other. You can ask them to point people to your page, and can do the same for them. This type of linking with other pages will give you the easy opportunity to gain views where you might have otherwise never found them.

Linking with a variety of other pages will make sure that even if you are not the lucky page clicked, eyes will still have a chance of seeing your page.

Google Adwords

Another way to drive traffic to your site is to use Google Adwords. When using Google Adwords, show the searcher that your ad is relevant. Google will display the search keywords in bold in your ad if they're present. This helps your ad stand out from the crowd.

Instead of having a single ad group with a large list of keywords, create many ad groups, each with a short list. Google's ad system determines placement by both bid and CTR (click through rate). To earn a high CTR, you first need to generate some clicks. Bid high initially so your ad is seen early in the search results. Once you have a high CTR, lower your bids.

If you set your daily budget too low, your ad will be displayed intermittently. This is not what you want. You always want your ad to be shown when someone searches for your keywords. Control your ad spend through other means such as employing negative keywords, using exact matches, targeting by region and adjusting keyword bids.

> *"Don't waste money getting into bidding wars..."*

Don't waste money getting into bidding wars for a handful of high volume keywords. Instead, expand your keyword list to include more specific keywords that have a lower search volume. Collectively, these keywords will reach the search volume of more expensive keywords. Your average CPC (cost per click) will fall dramatically using this tactic. Use keyword research tools to expand your list of keyword phrases.

Your ad will not be displayed if the search includes a negative keyword. Add more negative keywords at regular intervals. As your negative keyword list grows, your ad group's CTR will increase, saving you money and/or improving your ad's position. For example, if you sell products or services at a premium, include negative keywords like:

- free
- cheap
- discount

For most searches, don't point the ad to your home page. Choose a landing page on your site that includes the keywords from the search. In some cases, it's worth creating a custom page that's not in the normal navigation of your site.

Many people lose money using AdWords when their site is swamped with hits from content ads. Most people don't realise that displaying ads on Google's content network is turned on by default. Either turn off the content network or create separate campaigns for search and content ads.

Take advantage of Google's feature allowing multiple ads to be created and rotated within a single ad group. Test different ad text and see which version works best, both from an ROI and CTR perspective. A better ad will lead to a higher CTR and lower bids for the same ad position.

Viral and Buzz Marketing

Perhaps an underutilised method of marketing, viral and buzz methods allow you to connect to clients and customers without even creating online content. Truly free and essentially organic, buzz marketing is done by word of mouth. This method of marketing allows you to spread the word about your page and gets people curious enough to see what all of the fuss is about.

You can create a viral marketing campaign by pushing your page through a client or product in a populated area. You could go somewhere that your product is in high demand and find a place where there will be parties interested in looking up your page.

You can post signs and posters and tell as many people as you can about your page. This can be as simple as telling all of your Facebook friends to go like your page, announcing it to new acquaintances, telling people at work meetings or parties and having them spread the word simply by telling other people.

If your page is good and people find it interesting, the word will get around organically and you can use this advantage to find free followers for your page. This type of marketing may not always catch on, but if you have the right catch or the right page, it can start with a spark and spread like wildfire.

These methods can take very little effort, but can increase your views in big communities by large numbers. You will be getting results for very little effort and the number of people viewing your page can jump exponentially.

You can't do it all by yourself. Don't be afraid to rely on others to help you accomplish your goals.

Oprah Winfrey

Billionaire talk-show host

CHAPTER 8

Building Your Business Team

Chapter 8
Building Your Business Team

The financial success of your business will depend on your team (if you choose to enlist one) so look to build a strong team to ensure that your business does not die a quick death Struggling by yourself is not always the best idea. Sure it might make you a better-rounded businessman and may provide higher profits. However, it may not be the best idea if you are trying to accomplish things quickly, efficiently and effectively.

As your business team is an next essential part of your business, choose your team carefully and with an eye for people you can trust and count on and people that will produce the highest level of quality. When you are looking for your team, you should find people that are either experts in your field, or experts in the fields that you are recruiting them for, and you need to know how to serve as a boss to these employees.

> *"...choose your team carefully..."*

There are few people who can complete every aspect of the business process and you should know your limitations when it comes to these things. Completing every part of the process will force you to have knowledge of the niche, of writing, of blogging, search engine optimisation, design, software, website building and many other aspects, and sometimes this can simply be too much for one person to know or do.

You have the opportunity to enlist a trusted team, and allowing your team to have a common vision or goal gives them an opportunity to bond and develop a team spirit. The more people you get on board, the more impressive and creative minds that you have, the higher your opportunity for success will be. Your ability to earn a profit will be greater than you ever realised it to be.

Why You Need A Team

1. You will get more done faster

   With your team, you will be able to accomplish more than you ever have, and quicker than you ever have. If you hire experts in their field, they will be able to do something quicker than a non-expert would.

   If your business is structured properly, things will move faster. The more clearly defined each person's roles and responsibilities are, the easier it is for each person to be part of unit that works easily and cohesively together to streamline processes. Often problems tend to arise when it is not clear to people what they are meant to do and where their responsibilities lie.

   Every new person on board will take on new responsibilities, and their areas will all be specialised and completed with the utmost care and ability. The different skills will make the whole of the product better in the end.

2. Expert quality

Not only will you be able to do things more quickly with a team of workers, but you will be able to accomplish them at a higher, more polished level. With a whole team of specialised workers, you will have the ability to make every separate aspect of your product perfect. These specialised professionals can focus solely on what they are good at, and with this time invested, they will be able to accomplish the things that you may not have been able to do yourself.

Customer satisfaction may also grow due to your use of experts, as users will have fewer problems accessing your website, will have more people to contact and will be able to rely on fully polished and professional products in all aspects of your business.

You can make more money by not employing experts; say, by employing students or people with slight experience in the field, but this will not yield the best results. While you will pay more for quality, you will also see the best results from the most professional associates, coworkers and team members.

3. More support and more fun

Having people around can be better for obvious and natural reasons – and reasons that any person can enjoy. A larger team, especially if you are working from an office or home, will provide more opportunities for creative interaction and regular interpersonal interaction. The fun you can have working with your team can be an improvement over the atmosphere of simply working by yourself.

When you feel frustrated and ready to throw in the towel, you have your team to support you, to give you input and to bounce ideas off.

This open outlet for communication will give you the chance to benefit from a group of creative minds, instead of just your own, and the results will be apparent in the product. No longer will you have to worry about getting stuck – your only problem will be having too much fun and getting distracted.

Seeing business like a game can bring out your competitive juices and make you more inclined to produce more, make more money and set up the best business possible – all with the advantage of a team to help create this "winning" attitude.

4. Larger available network

Working with a group of people like this will also put you in the best possible position to find more professionals, more customers and more clients. With a team of say six or eight, each person will have their own circle of contacts. And, within each person's circle, you may find someone who has additional skills or talents.

Your business should not be established as an island and you should always have open doors for additional people to join your team. Through your team's contact you are also in a position to market your business further, sharing information with the networking circle of each person in your team. With one team member's contacts, you might even find a broad client list, another group of customers, or even someone willing to connect with your business for a mutually agreeable joint venture.

5. More money

While many may think that they would like to cut their team to allow themselves higher profits, this can be faulty logic. Often the truth is, when you have a team with a number of valuable members, you will be creating more content and more profits and the money you are sharing will be greater than the money that you might have been able to make by yourself.

The Team acronym – Together Everybody Achieves More – is never more true than in business. Sometimes you need to give a little to gain a little more.

> *"The Team acronym – Together Everybody Achieves More ..."*

Structuring Your Team

You can structure your team in a variety of ways, but the following are some of the most common and most useful ways of doing so:

1. Employees

Like a typical department store, business corporation or fast food restaurant, hiring employees for your business can be good for a number of reasons. This is the typical working model, and gathering a base of employees under you to work in an office environment can be one way of getting people to creatively interact with each other.

This allows you to get long term commitment from your employees, but it can end up being expensive. If you have to pay employees to work for you, you will likely have to pay them whether you business is successful or not. You will also have a number of legal and tax responsibilities in regards to your employees and this can end up becoming difficult to track.

If you have employees on an hourly rate, you may not be getting your money's worth, as many employees are not working the entire time that they are at the office. While it can be good for someone with a large payroll and a lot of work, this option will not be great for everyone.

2. Outsourcing

Outsourcing is another popular option that will allow you to get jobs accomplished faster than if you decided to do them yourself. With outsourcing there is already a precedent set in the Internet industry, as this is one of the major ways that people are employed for Internet businesses.

This can also add the advantage (or disadvantage) of having workers in different time zones. If you can set up the jobs correctly, you can have a person in the first time zone complete their part of the project, and then pass it off to the next time zone and so on. If you end in your time zone as the last stop of the project, you can have your work completely done by the time you start your work day, instead of wasting an entire day waiting for the content to get completed.

This can also be a disadvantage as you may have different working hours, and even sleeping hours, than the people that you are working with. While it can allow you to move your business at high speeds, you must judge this against the need for having your work done at certain times, and pick people not only for their qualifications and rates, but for their time zones as well.

Another problem with outsourcing is that you may run into a variety of people that are less than reliable or less than qualified. These people can slow down a job, as they can overestimate their portfolios or capabilities, and you may find yourself going through a few unsuccessful hired helpers before you meet one that you like.

This can cost money as you are wasting time and potentially paying for unwanted content and you might also be taking on other people's work as you find yourself correcting the work already done by the people you've outsourced to.

Sometimes outsourcing can end up being very costly, as well, especially if you are outsourcing to high end professionals.

With outsourced work, there is also no guarantee of a long-term relationship. Those that you outsource to may simply be interested in a one-and-done job or it may be hard to keep track of them over weeks or months. They may change their price, their situation may change and there may be no way to make them complete your work on the schedules that you would like them to.

If they are only interested in being paid at the end of the month, the quality may not be as high as it could be otherwise. If they are simply out for cash you need to know that they are not invested in your company and they will not gain financially from doing extra work on your projects as they will be finished with any involvement with you or your company after the current job is completed.

Contractors

Contractors are generally professionals in their field and often have reputations based on quality service, but they also may not always provide the best opportunities for your business. Like outsourced workers, they are not invested in your company and the quality of their work can suffer because of this.

Short-term contracts might be carried out at the same time that they are working with chief competitors and they may be holding out better work for the higher paying company. Also, if they see something they like within your framework, they may bring that to their next job to reap larger rewards and to impress a paying employer. All of these can take away from the esteem, quality and uniqueness of your product. A slippery slope indeed, contract work can be a mutually beneficial experience, but it must be embarked upon with an eye for quality, the right person and the right job.

Joint Ventures

Joint ventures can be among the safest and best possibilities for getting work done, for both parties. With a joint venture, both sides will have to work hard to make money and there is no up front cost involved with this arrangement.

Payment is based on results and partnering up with someone means that you are both interested in the same goals and will both be pursuing these ends to a profit. In the joint venture arrangement if you do not succeed they do not succeed and vice versa. If you are both professionals looking to use each other to help your own success, and offer your help for their success, the agreement will be mutually agreeable and you may be able to make more profits this way than you ever could have without that partner.

In some circumstances, however, it can cost more in the long term. If you have a deal and you are splitting profits down the middle, you may lose out if your section of the business is obviously drawing in a higher percentage of the profits. In the same vein, though, if they are drawing in more of the profits, you will benefit from having made your 50/50 agreement.

There are no absolute rules as to what will be best for your business, but you can analyze your options, your business and your products to determine what might be the best for you. With this kind of information you can get to the bottom of how you should run your business and choose in which way to engage those that will become your team.

Hybridise Your Team

An important part at the beginning of the process will be hybridising your team. While you may need to utilise simple contractors or outsourced work at the beginning of the process, you should quickly be able to network to find people that are out to benefit your business. You will soon have more resources and more income and will be able to decide precisely how you want your team run.

Your best bet is to use a combination of all of the team options and find the situation that works the best for each area of your business. This will give you the freedom to do whatever is best with each section and will allow you to save money, make money and supply your business with the best team possible.

You can also search for an automated answer to your problem before outsourcing it to another worker, as this will save you money in the long run. You should always do your research to know how much an amount of work should cost and what kind of quality to expect as well.

Recruiting Your Team

The next essential step of the process is actually getting the different members of your team on board. But how do you recruit people for your team? This can be an easy process for some and more difficult for others.

Like every other step of the business process, you must first immerse yourself in research. You must know exactly what you are looking for, exactly how much you can pay and exactly what kind of quality you expect. You must know the different kinds of people, and you must know what they bring to the table.

Of the two different kinds of workers you might encounter, the first has an entrepreneurial nature and will likely be in for gaining over the long term. They are success-oriented and are looking for results in exchange for putting in time and effort. They will make great partners and will be interested in the future success of the business.

The other type of worker, much less desirable, will be into short-term results. These people are often contractors and will not be out to further your company. These people will be interested in completing the current job and moving on to their next outlet. Their main goal will be getting done and getting paid – putting your job behind them – so that they can move onto their next quick buck.

You need to find workers that are committed. You can test their commitment from the beginning by putting the interview in an odd place or time and making them really show that they care about the job. They may not be into doing something out of the ordinary if they are not committed and you should make sure that you test them to see if they really are in it for the long haul.

You should also test their attitude and skill. Some people have skills that are taught and some people are naturally good at things and you need to find the kind of people whose skills will work well in your day to day business. This doesn't necessarily mean qualifications, as not every skilled person will have gone to college, had an internship or had previous experience with a high paycheck.

All you need to know is whether a person is skilled or not and you can find this out through samples of their work and through talking to them generally about their knowledge of and interest in a subject.

You should also discover what a person's other commitments are. You need to determine if they are willing to put full time work into your company, if required, and, if not, you need to figure out what might keep them from putting their time into your company. You should know their availability and discover how easy it will be to communicate to them. You need to find someone who is interested in going above and beyond in the future, if required, and you can do all of this by giving them an eye for your workload. Ask them how long it would take to do a particular job and you discover from them how long that they have taken to complete similar projects in the past.

Can they work well in a team? This is one of the other important aspects of any teammate and one that may or may not be evident on the surface. If the person you are looking at can work well in a team it can enhance the look, feel and attitude of your company and it will allow you to trust someone who is truly interested in putting out the best product possible, helping others to do the same and watching the business succeed in general.

Another requirement for someone on your team is a shared vision. Whoever you are hiring should enjoy the same enthusiasm for the project as you and be someone who is willing to see the same vision and results as you. They must fully understand how you are trying to carry out the project and they must be able to creatively agree and add to this vision. They must understand the common goal and this shared outcome should be their driving force, just like it is with you and every other member of your team.

Your employees must also be passionate about the product or business that you are selling. A passionate employee will be willing to work and will not need to be forced into doing anything. These people will often work for less pay, be devoted to the company and will be the most interested in putting in the work for the sake of the profit, the product and the team.

Speed and quality of communication is important. Your employees must realise how important it is to stay in constant contact with you and that you would like to keep these lines of communication open at all times, especially on short notice. There are a variety of communication methods that your employees should be well versed in (eg, email, telephone,etc) and they should assure you that they will be able to communicate through these outlets as often as is possible and whenever required.

> *Money gives you the freedom to do with your time what you want to do with it.*

Richard Branson

Virgin Group - Billionaire

CHAPTER 9

Building Your Cost Effective
Website That Sells

Chapter 9
Building Your Cost Effective Website That Sells

Building your own website is an essential part of the process of having your own Internet business and there are various resources that allow you to do this. WordPress and FusionHQ are two of the most commonly used systems and these have both become very popular because of the ease of with which they can be learnt and used.

While you can outsource the creation of your website, this can cost as much as a few thousand dollars, especially if you are expecting top of the line features, graphics and designs. With tools like WordPress and FusionHQ, spending this money has become simply unnecessary and you have all the tools at your disposable to make the website yourself. You will be able to make it both usable and professional looking and most visitors will not know the different between a professionally made site and one constructed using a tool like FusionHQ. You can create all different types of sites, from sales sites to membership sites, and can use these to partner with your business or other businesses, or to advertise your products.

You can create a very sophisticated looking site – and one that operates with a level of sophistication – all while having no previous knowledge of programming languages. This will mean you can forego studying and learning the confusing HTML or CSS scripts and characters. You will have the technology in front of you and you can use this technology to generate whatever kind of web content it is that you are looking for.

FusionHQ

FusionHQ is a site-builder in itself and it makes building your own site easier than it has ever been. While HTML, CSS and other programming languages will force you to precisely install scripts and characters to design your webpage, FusionHQ does not require this. You are simply left to decide and choose which objects you would like on your site and then add them. If, for example, you would like to put an advertisement or sales feature on the page, you can do this with no inherent knowledge of the programming language required to do so.

If you are trying to add a "Buy Now" or "Add to Cart" button to your website, you can add these to your page in just a few clicks with FusionHQ. This site is utilised through dropping and dragging methods and you will easily be able to edit the website after you have finished. With other website development tools you have to worry about messing up the HTML programming language if you are trying to edit, but this is not the case with FusionHQ. The webpage can be altered and the old scripts will remain in place – the new ones will simply be added in addition.

With no experience in web design, this tool gives you the chance to customise your lay-out and design and to arrange and rearrange all of the items on your webpage at will. The official website of FusionHQ even offers step-by-step instructions to lead you through the process of setting up your webpage. In addition, built in securities on the website protect your download links from spam and they provide you with codes to make sure that you are the only person who will be able to control your newly created website.

With FusionHQ, you can also link to your PayPal.com page.. While PayPal buttons are not the most difficult buttons to make through

HTML, FusionHQ quickens the process through their own Process Wizard. This application gives you the chance to provide information about your product's payment plan..

You will be able to choose one-time payment methods and you can also set the price. You can divide one payment into multiple payments and choose the terms on which you will be paid.

Through the website you can also provide programs, webinars or other products that you can charge a subscription fee for and you can set and sell plans to any of your customers and clients. You can determine plans and payment options for these subscriptions and then add easy cancel buttons for your customers to get out of the subscription.

You can offer your customer's a "free trial period," or you can charge them right away. With these options available you are free to choose how you are going to conduct your business, what decisions you will give your customers and how you are going to make money.

With the creation of a membership site, using FusionHQ, you can simply select your membership template and create the additional elements for the page – including headers, new pages and internal and external links. You can choose whether your page can be accessed by the public or only by registered users with passwords and access. You can then decide how long content is released for and what the wait is before the content is made available. These easy options let you select exactly what content is meant for what users – or for what level of user.

Like any good website builder, FusionHQ also allows you the ability to insert text content, insert images and even host videos to your website. In just a few seconds, your visitors can be enjoying a video that you can control through various playback options. They will then also be able to control how the video is viewed on their screen. You can edit d and quality options, and you can set you can set up features like these to your own personal specifications.

The FusionHQ software continues to add capabilities as the site grows in both size and capabilities and there are a variety of new features that you can now utilise when creating your websites.

You can add upsell, downsell and squeeze pages to add variety to your site and you can incorporate exit pop-ups and thank you pages as well. In a simple process you are able to setup your entire sales process and funnel on professional-looking pages.

You can fully integrate your page with ClickBack, 1ShoppingCart and Authorize.net, in addition to PayPal, and you can engage in affiliate management easily. With these features you can run a self-managed program if desired. You are also able to use auto-responder programs like Aweber, GetResponse and iContact in conjunction with FusionHQ.

Other options include auto opt-in for customers and clients, as well as different lists included for each purchase, product and customer. The membership setup can be completed in just minutes and you can release content by date, by increment or by length of time.

With fully customisable templates, you can borrow from existing pages and add your own personal touch to them. You can duplicate your website and sales process and put it on auto-drive. This automation will ease the money-making process and allow you more time to pursue other interests as the sales continue to pile in.

Another feature allows you to insert custom snippets of code, if they are not available on FusionHQ, and this allows you to add professionally made javascript codes, iframes or embedded documents.

You can track how your site is doing with a resource like Google Analytics and you can control this manually or automatically. With fast response from FusionHQ customer service you can keep your site up and running if there are problems.

There are also frequent updates and down-period maintenance changes to keep the site from having any problems and development and beta testing enhancements that have the site integrated like WordPress, but operating at a different level.

In our opinion FusionHQ is at the leading edge when it comes to new easy to use web building software and its brilliant for people who want all the key marketing components built into the software.

To find out more visit http://www.FusionHQ.com/package/internet-secrets-revealed-book/

WordPress

Similar to FusionHQ, WordPress is another popular option for users of website-building software, programs or sites. WordPress is more of a blogging site, but allows you to host your own page with easy to use schematics and a number of professional looking specifications and design features.

With WordPress, you have the opportunity to create your layouts and templates, add your own features and additions, and access these all without having to worry about the more confusing aspects of HTML, CSS and programming languages – just like FusionHQ.

The WordPress website started as a program used for bloggers, but has become a legitimate way of creating your own website for other purposes. By basing everything off of a homepage you can do the same kind of site-building that will allow you to customise every single aspect of your site. Buttons are more difficult, and design is not as advanced, but WordPress will also allow you to add any kind of media and will give you the chance to customise text, images, banners, outlines and many other features.

WordPress, as a content management system, features a magazine layout that has become popular for many. It allows you to define custom content and is a popular resource for pages specialising in search engine optimisation. It is a type of open source software and runs on PHY/MySQL interfaces. It can be edited with easy clicks of the mouse, and the themes on the website will maintain a level of consistency between your different features, all without you doing any work yourself. It will look like a regular website, not a blog, and the plug-ins available for the site give you a great opportunity to mesh with other paginating features.

While not as capable as FusionHQ, WordPress is a popular alternative for slightly simpler sites.

Because you are doing most of the other work on the business in-house, or completing it yourself, why not save money and complete this part of the job yourself as well. Of the two websites, FusionHQ is the more technologically advanced, but WordPress, on the other hand, is slightly simpler, but will not provide the fancier and more professional look that you might be looking for – especially if you are running a membership website.

Money gives you the freedom to do with your time what you want to do with it.

Richard Branson
Virgin Group - Billionaire

CHAPTER 10

Social Media Marketing
Success Strategies

Chapter 10
Social Media Marketing Success Strategies

Facebook is no longer simply a novelty or a simple site for college and high school networking buddies. It is a revolution – a business tool, an exercise in effective marketing and even a major motion picture. It has transcended other uses of the Internet and has become a major form of communication for middle schoolers to Fortune 500 companies.

Maybe unexplainable to some, the reality is that Facebook is undeniably one of the largest outlets of communication in the world. Using the same tenets that established the Internet as a marketing tool, the social networking website has exploded in growth and importance lately.

> **"... Facebook is undeniably one of the largest outlets of communication in the world."**

One of the top two most visited sites on the Internet, Facebook trails on Google, and is quickly expanding to reach out for that top spot. The networking website has recently expanded its brand and capabilities to make marketing easier, more effective and more profitable for businesses – both large and small – from across the globe.

Facebook fan pages are used for products, good and services, and can be used to make your business popular. These pages are meeting places for consumers, customers, clients, employees and workers and allow you to wield an incredible influence within your page.

Allowing for free marketing, the Facebook fan page allows you to reach out to an audience of millions, many of whom are spending half of their day on the networking website. For businesses with Facebook fan pages, one of the key words to any owner is "Like."

The "Like" button is a tab on the top of the page and allows for the easiest method of virally marketing between users. When any user clicks the "Like" button on your business page, the like action will show up on the pages of all of that user's friends. This will then be noticed by all of this person's other friends, which can number as many as several hundred or in the low thousands.

The more friends that "Like" your page, the more times a person will be exposed to the name and they may quickly become interested enough to check out your page.

This free form of viral marketing can quickly turn into a tool that will have your business, product or good on the tongues – and Facebook pages – of users and potential customers and clients around the world.

Creating an Interesting and Exciting Page

Perhaps more important to your page than any other single factor to your "Likes" is creating a page that people will both enjoy and find useful. The only way to get people on your page – and keep them coming back – is to have a page that is both interesting and exciting. It needs to be unique to get people clicking the "Like" button and this will drive followers to your page every time.

An interesting page should be well-designed and well-organised and should have all of the essential features of a Facebook page. Your business page should include an exciting profile picture that best shows off your business or products, and this should be complimented by other profile pictures. Interesting and exciting can be had in a variety of ways and will depend on your product.

The rise of Facebook

Active users, millions

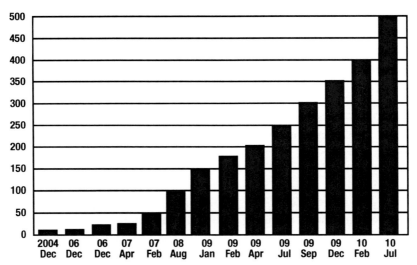

Source: Facebook

Growth of Facebook

Sex always sells and so does humor, but this will be dictated by your brand. Professionalism and a clear, polished look will sell to many others and no one will understand your client base better than you.

In addition to grabbing attention with your profile picture, you should make sure the layout of your page is engaging to readers, followers and visitors. Your posts should be succinct, clear, concise and to the point. They should get readers excited about what you are doing with your page and your business.

Your posts should make large announcements, tell followers about exciting deals and events, and serve to get them exciting about your business. This can be done with exciting pictures, personal posts from favorite employees and news about sales and deals. The only way to get buzz for your business is to create it yourself, and you should use every tool at your disposal to do so.

You can outsource work on your page to add banners and other flashy attachments. If you have a larger budget, a professional can give you the opportunity to spice up the look of your page and it will then be up to you to add the kind of content that is both exciting and interesting.

How To Be Useful To Your Followers

The Facebook pages that get the most attention are the ones that are the most useful to their followers. These pages should give everyone that "Likes" your page a reason to stick around and further reasons to continue visiting every week or every day.

Useful pages will have all of the information needed for a business. You will have to link to your homepage, send other relevant links and keep updating the page on a normal schedule.

While quality should not be forsaken for quantity, you should update your page at least every other day. The updates on your page need to be fresh, interesting and relevant. For example, if you own a Civil War memorabilia company, your posts need to update your followers of new items, new deals and new ways to buy and trade.

You should establish yourself as an authority on the subject and make your posts include content that you can only see on your Facebook page. Having exclusive content will make users have to come to your page to get what they are looking for.

Include pictures of your products, and allow visitors to get things that other pages will not provide. In this way you will be rewarding your followers. You should give people an incentive to come to your page and common updates with good information will have them wanting to like your page.

If you are a baking company, make normal posts with cooking hints. While this may be outside of the scope of a certain product you are selling, they can be entertaining and useful for followers, and give them a reason to check your page every couple hours.

Being useful to your followers will make them more likely to click the "Like" button on your page. Once the button is clicked, the buzz will spread, and your followers will increase as you see the results piling up.

Original content should be well thought out, and you should never forsake quality for usefulness. Be timely as well. If there is news in your industry, be the first to announce it, and let followers get things through your page that they cannot even get on your website.

Posting Content

As already mentioned, the content on your page needs to be fresh, original and professional – but it should also be consistent and competent.

Blow is a graphic that shows the different elements you should have when designing your website or social media marketing

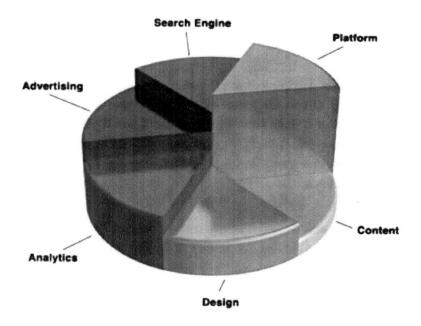

Social Marketing Pie

If you are advertising for a comedy lounge or a particular act, your content should reflect this. Post dates and times where you will be playing, advertise ticket prices, tell your fans where to come see you and encourage them to be different.

Give them bios of your comedy team on your page. Tell them things that they will not find out elsewhere. These pages are often for people who are serious about you or your product and you should use this to get people interested and keep them excited.

Post every day and don't keep followers guessing. The kind of content you post will have a large effect on how many clicks you get and may even allow you to reap the rewards of word-of-mouth buzz.

> *"... reap the rewards of word-of-mouth buzz."*

You should also post content at the correct times to take advantage of your following. If you are appealing to a 25-39 year old crowd that is up late, post your content between 10 pm and 2 am. If you are catering to an older group that is likely on their computers early, post between 5 am and 10 am. You should know your following and know when they are on their computers.

Facebook use tends to spike in the evenings, around 7 pm when people are off work and studying for school. It is also at its highest on the weekend when people are home and surfing the Internet. Post at these busy times to make sure that your posts get seen. With your post showing up in news feeds, followers are more likely to interact with you. If they interact, this will appear on the feeds of your follower's friends, and they will notice your page as well.

Videos and Links

Videos and links are a way of incorporating the most interesting content on your page and to get people interested and excited unlike any other form of content. Just like YouTube.com has enjoyed an incredible popularity, as well as Vevo.com, these tools can be used to address the short attention spans of users and followers.

> **"If you are promoting your band, place actual videos on your page..."**

If you are promoting your band, place actual videos on your page of a performance or recent show. Film yourself traveling or goofing around, and allow your fans to connect to your band. Create an advertisement for your band using a few friends.

Your video content should be funny, shocking or exciting. Like the videos on YouTube that get the most views, odd or exciting content will get people laughing or gasping and will drive visitors to your page in droves larger than ever before.

You can easily film your own videos with cameras or even with your phone, and upload to sites like YouTube. You can then click the "Video" tab on your page and share these with your followers. These often produce the most comments and buzz from followers.

Like videos, you can also use links to create excitement for your page. The links should be, like all other content, useful or exciting. You should give your followers exclusive links to your products, links to employee's personal pages, links to articles about your brand or links to reviews of whatever you are doing.

These videos and these links will not only enhance your ability to help and reward your viewer and followers, but will give you the opportunity to share other content from across the Web. In addition to increasing the buzz on your page, you can also get people to buy from your other websites, to draw traffic to your blog or even to follow your Twitter page.

This kind of attention can only be gleaned from content that is highly original and exciting. The videos could be a direct plea to your Facebook followers and you can even use this method as a shameless ploy to get them to tell their friends to increase your likes.

Finding Followers

Finding followers can be one of the more difficult ways of getting likes, but it can be done in a variety of ways. You can start by using Facebook's normal search tools to discover people that are interested in your brand or in your product.

You can enter certain search items, such as "baseball equipment", into the main search bar on the top of your Facebook page. After clicking "Enter," you will see a list of results of people that have used the phrase or might be interested in it. Select from these people to invite to your page.

You can also seek out similar brands and pages, and invite from the "Like" list. Click on the page of a different baseball equipment company and notice all of the users that have followed their page. Send messages to these users, or click on one follower and invite them to "Like" your page.

You can also search baseball websites and forum pages, and try to find forums that link to each poster's Facebook page.

Another effective way of finding followers is by simply engaging in as much activity as possible. You should also friend other people in your industry. If someone else is following the page that you friend, they may notice the new friendship on their Facebook feed, and see that your page is related to their interest. If this is the case, they could easily click on your page and do a little looking around.

Using Facebook Advertising

Facebook advertising is popular for a number of different reasons. It allows you to advertise a number of different things, and though you may have to pay a small fee to advertise, it is likely that this will be one of your company's most visible advertisements through any medium.

> *"... over 300 million Facebook users..."*

You are given the opportunity to reach over 300 million Facebook users, attach social actions to your ads and create demand for your product. You will be creating advertisements that are either image based or text based and you can advertise web pages or even something else on your Facebook page.

You can track your ad's progress with real-time reporting and get insight as to the kind of people that are accessing your ads and then make modifications to them to maximise your results.

To access your ads, click "Advertising" on the bottom of any page on your Facebook account.

Take a few minutes to gather some items you'll need to create your Facebook Ad:

- A link that your ad will be advertising. Decide whether you want to advertise your own web page or something on Facebook like a Page, Application, Group or Event.

- Write a message that is clear and concise. They should be targeted ads with concise text that speaks directly to the audience you will reach. The title can have up to 25 characters, and the body can have up to 135 characters.

- Also, prepare a photograph that is attractive and relevant in your ad. It should be appropriate for the product or service being advertised. The image will be resized to fit in a 110px wide by 80px high box.

The following steps will take you through the creation of your ad, using the following Facebook advertising page.

The above is the page that you will be met with once you click the "Advertising" tab on the bottom of the screen. This page will give you an overview of the advertising process. Next, click "Create an Ad" on the top right corner, where you will be given a chance to upload creative content, including a title for your ad (up to 25 characters in length including spaces) and content for the body of your ad (up to 135 characters in length including spaces) in the space provided. As you are creating your ad, a preview of it will be shown to you.

You may also upload a photo or image, but this is optional.

Your ads should be written in a way that is catchy and that will catch the eye and the ear of your potential buyers. If you are unsure of what to write, take a few minutes to look at the ads that others have written and use these as an example. You can also look at the pastel back-shaded sponsored listings ads at the top of any Google search page.

You then must decide whether you want people to be directed to your own web page or something on Facebook like a Page, Application, Group or Event. If you are already the administrator of your Facebook Page, Group, Event, or Application, you can select it from the drop down option.

In this step, you may also choose to precisely target by age, gender, location and more. If you check the box, we will add content that notifies a user of their friends' interactions with your brand or business on Facebook. More information about social actions can be found on the Facebook FAQ section.

Next, you should target your audience. Do this with demographic and psychographic filters about real people. By default, Facebook targets all users 18 and older in the default location.

Use the drop down menus to select what kind of audience you would like to target, including age, birthday, sex, relationships and connections. You should appeal to certain groups of people who would most likely be interested in your product or site.

However, you are encouraged to modify this to reach the most appropriate people for your ad. Be sure to reference the approximate reach figure for an estimate of the number of people who match your criteria.

On this "Campaigns and Pricing" screen you will denote what currency you want your payments in, you will give your campaign a name and you will have to decide how much money you are willing to spend on Facebook advertising per day.

There is no set cost for Facebook Ads, but you can estimate the cost for your ads in the ad creation interface. We recommend you bid for each click (CPC) or thousand impressions (CPM), just enter your targeting criteria and then going through to Step 4 of ad creation (you won't have to enter any payment information until the next step, so you can do this without purchasing an ad).

The "bid estimator" will show you the range of bids that are currently winning the auction among ads similar to yours. Based on this, you can determine how much you wish to spend per click or per thousand impressions. The cost per click or CPM associated with an ad, along with the ad quality, influences how often it is shown.

If you decide to use CPC bear in mind that you will only pay when someone actually clicks on your add with the intent of buying your products or services regardless of how many times you add has been viewed.

If you decide to use the CPM you pay every time someone sees/views your add regardless if they click on it or not. In general, using the CPC is a much more profitable method for selling products and services, unless you are a very well known brand like Coca Cola or Ford and you are doing the advertising for brand awareness; then CPM will make more sense.

Of course there are exceptions to the rule. The more you are able to bid for clicks or impressions the better your positioning will be and the better your exposure will be which means an increase in profits.

When you have completed all the fields, click "Create" at the bottom of the page and you will be met with the following screen, where you can double check your ad and insert your payment details.

All ads go through a quality review prior to being shown. Ads are reviewed to ensure that they meet content guidelines.

If you require further information you can refer to the advertising guidelines on the payment page.

You will then be able to view your ads progress within hours. Your click through rate (CTR) is a particularly good indicator of how well your ads are doing. You can also view your clicks, impressions and average CPC or CPM by checking your account.

Allow your ad performance to educate you about effective strategies for achieving your goals. As you observe your ads over time, you might notice things that are working especially well (or not so well).

**To Get a <u>FREE copy</u> of an ebook called
<u>"Facebook Marketing Secrets"</u> simply visit this website link
www.DarrenJStephens.com/facebook-marketing-secrets**

Internet Marketing

While, for your purposes, the Facebook page itself is being used as one large Internet marketing tool, the broader Internet itself can be used as well.

The Internet allows you to reach an audience larger than any other outlet and there are ways online to get buzz for your page unlike any other marketing channel.

If you are a person who sends off a lot of emails – whether you are emailing to clients, consumers, potential partners or customers – you should include a link to your Facebook page in your signature.

You should seek out forums and message boards that discuss your product, brand or service. You should make voluntary posts in these boards and use your posts to plug your Facebook page.

You should also, obviously, use your own brand's website to plug your Facebook page. Place links for your page on your website, and include a "Like" button on your website so followers can click the link without even leaving your webpage. These links give you the opportunity to promote your page from outside of Facebook.

You should use professional websites like LinkedIn to add a "Link" tab to your Facebook page and you can use other social networking sites like MySpace and FriendFeed to promote your page as well. All of these resources can get people clicking on your page and clicking the "Like" button to find relevant and important content.

With these opportunities to post across the Internet, you could spend hours getting free marketing for your page. People will be noticing your name and your brand more than ever before and, even if they are not clicking on your "Like" the first time they see your name, there is a chance you may get that click with the second, third or fourth notice.

Though not on the Internet, you can also promote your page inside your store's physical location, on letterheads, on business cards and even in advertisement magazines or coupons.

Twitter Marketing

Twitter marketing is becoming one of the new revolutions in Internet marketing and is often complementary with facebook marketing. Twitter is a sort of simplified version of Facebook, and allows you to reach followers in many other inventive ways.

Twitter actually features an application that allows you to link the two accounts. With the two accounts lined, any post you make on your Twitter will show up on your Facebook page and any post made on Facebook will show up on your Twitter home page.

You can find a bevy of visitors and followers through Twitter's search capabilities, which are more useful and extensive than Facebook's. With the Twitter search tools, you can simply enter a word and find users that have been tweeting about the same subjects. You can then add these people to your page and send them private or bulk messages.

You can ask them to visit your Facebook page, ask them to like your page or allow them to direct you to other users that might be interested in your brand. There are nearly limitless ways to connect on Twitter and using your own keywords is another method that is both common and very effective.

Even without searching out other users yourself, you can find people by posting your own updates on your page. Post what you are selling or providing and people who are searching for the same things will find you. Write a short description and include a link to your Facebook page.

If you include "1960s records" in your tweet, along with a link to your Facebook page, you can easily connect to anyone searching for the same things. With millions of followers on Twitter, there is a good chance there will be users looking for that. Once they enter the search, your page will come up and they will have only to click on your page. You should post content on your Twitter page just like your Facebook page and put up clear and concise messages at least a few times per day.

Social Bookmarking

Social bookmarking can be an indispensable tool for anyone looking to create buzz for their Facebook page. This method of communication – similar to actual social networking – allows you to reach a broad audience that can create buzz from different websites.

Article directories and websites across the Internet allow you to post content for other viewers to enjoy. Like Facebook itself, these directories and bookmarking pages are meant for users to share with each other and are often fully customisable and fully searchable.

You can post links to your Facebook page on any bookmarking website and users who are interested in your content, product or brand will be able to find you based on this.

Along with your actual Facebook link, post an article, video or picture to get people interested. Ask for "Likes" on your page and use the video as you would a video on your actual page.

Make the content relevant, interesting and indispensable to the reader. Make it the kind of content that people will seek out and find interesting. It should mark you as an expert and propel followers to seek out your Facebook page directly and click that "Like" button to get automatic updates to your expertise and knowledge.

Blog Marketing

Blog marketing is another common way to get more clicks of the "Like" button on your Facebook page. When you are using blogs, you have the ability to speak directly to your followers and visitors and can make personal pleas like asking them to click your "Like" button. With blogs, the marketing has already been done and you already have a list of followers or visitors.

Compliment your Facebook page with your blog by simply making blog posts as you normally would and always incorporating links to your Facebook page. You can include clickable icons and "Like" buttons that allow followers to like your profile page without ever leaving the actual blog page.

The blog is important because you will likely already have established a client base and, if they are frequent visitors, they likely already trust you and your brand. There is also a good chance that they know a variety of other people in the same niche, or looking for the same product. If this is the case, make sure that you alert your followers of your blog to direct their friends to your Facebook page.

Encourage everyone to click like, and be sure that you are not duplicating content from page to page. If you have certain content on your Facebook page, make sure that your blog followers know that this content can not be found in other places.

This type of unique content – not found on your blog – makes your Facebook page an indispensable source of information for any potential followers and the only way to get consistent updates is by liking your page.

Viral and Buzz Marketing

Perhaps an underutilised method of "Like" marketing, viral and buzz methods allow you to connect to clients and customers without even creating online content. Truly free and essentially organic, buzz marketing is done by word of mouth. This method of marketing allows you to spread the word about your page and get curious people to see what all of the fuss is about.

You can create a viral marketing campaign by pushing your page through a client or product in a populated area. You should go somewhere that your product is in high demand and find a place where there will be parties interested in looking up your page.

You can post signs and posters and tell as many people as you can about "Like"-ing your page. This can be as simple as telling all of your Facebook friends to go like your page, announcing it to new acquaintances, telling people at work meetings or parties and having them spread the word simply by telling other people.

If your page is good and people find it interesting, the word will get around organically and you can use this advantage to find free followers for your page. This type of marketing may not always catch on, but if you have the right catch or the right page, it can start with a spark and spread like wildfire.

These methods can take very little effort and can increase your "Likes" in big communities by large numbers. You will be getting results for very little effort, and your page "Like" numbers will jump exponentially.

Buying Facebook "Likes"

While not the most cost effective way of getting Facebook "Likes", buying them can be the easiest and the quickest. This method allows you to generate buzz for your page by increasing the status of the page without any grass roots methods.

Companies sell "Like" packages that can be delivered to your page for dozens, hundreds or thousands of dollars. These "Likes" can be added to your page in days or in months, and some companies even offer "Likes" in the range of hundreds of thousands at a time.

Having this many likes on your page will increase the legitimacy of your profile and people will be more likely to click on it if they see your name and it interests them.

Hundreds or thousands of users make people believe that your page is both valuable and useful and having these users will draw other people to click on your page. If you have 250,000 likes and a similar page has only 10,000, your page will likely get more views because of the buzz around it.

The type of status levied by 250,000 likes can do wonders for a page that has a truly good product to sell or one that is advertising a product, good, service or act with true potential. Just like you can buy Twitter followers and blog comments, buying Facebook followers will give you a higher page ranking, more legitimacy and more success. Sellers of "Likes" include SocialKik, FacebookFans, Fanbullet and Fanpage Hookup.

Tagging and Participating

Activity is another key to succeeding and drawing "Likes" on Facebook, and will allow you to connect to other users. The most important kind of activities you can engage in are simply participating in the normal uses of Facebook.

If you are a band looking to get followers you should take pictures at your shows. You can also ask fans to sign up for your shows. After the show, upload your pictures and tag the people that showed up for the show. Create a note or a Facebook status with the names of people at the show and tag them in this post.

While these people probably already "Like" you and your Facebook page, other people likely will not. If you are tagging 10 people, each with 400 friends, you can be exposing your page to as many as 4,000 followers, just through 10 people.

Once you tag one of these ten people, the tag will show up in the News Feed of all their friends and they will be able to see the recognition and fun that they had at the show.

This will increase the liklihood of their friends clicking "Like" on your page and then you will continue branching out to larger and larger groups of expanding friends, followers and visitors.

Other types of participation include writing on people's walls, creating events, adding comments to pictures and links and adding friends through requests. All of these activities will get people noticing your page, and these can propel your "Likes" from the dozens to the hundreds or even thousands.

Reminding Followers

Though some may prefer not to do this, and others might think that it sounds annoying or irritating, reminding followers to get others to "Like" your page can be an important part of the process.

Through this method, you may get a few followers for each reminder and it will have taken only a few seconds of your time. You can promise your followers a certain nugget of information, a deal or a special surprise if you reach a certain number of "Likes."

This will likely work to encourage them to tell others to "Like" your page and, with a surprise announced, the new people will then, in-turn, alert others to get your page even more notice.

Just make sure your reminders do not sound like begging. You can remind people to "Like" your page in pictures that have high comment levels – this way everyone that commented might see your reminder. You can send people personal messages in bulk or you can post on their pages to get them to add followers.

You can even throw in the reminder as an aside for a normal message. Your message could tell your fans of a recent deal and you can add a reminder to the end to influence them to reward your service with word of mouth advertising.

Expand Your Profile

This personal information can be important for clients if you are a single business owner. If you are starting a page for a large group or a corporation, simply add the contact information and location.

The different things that you put on your Facebook page should represent your business in the best way possible. The details should include only and all details that will paint your business in the best light possible.

You must be sure to include as much contact information as possible, and give your viewers a chance to link with other customers and examples of your work.

Your links, events, applications, pages and your wall say a lot about what it is that you are doing with your page and your business and the content that you display on your page can go a long way in generating for you the kind of profits that you desire.

Before examining the more profitable marketing aspects of Facebook, as well as the various applications that can be used for different things, you should first realise how to use your "publisher" and post things to your wall.

Your wall is a large space of free marketing that you can make available to an enormous list of people and it should be used as such.

Your wall is the area on your page that is first seen when someone visits your page. This is the section of your page that is the most versatile and gives you the largest chance to publish almost anything that you want.

Your wall can be used for placing links, videos, pictures, notes, events or your own words, thoughts or ideas.

Linking With Other Pages

Linking with other pages can be another indispensable tool that can allow you to achieve the kind of results that you are looking for. By linking to other pages, and allowing other pages to link to you, you can create a mutually beneficial relationship with other pages and other businesses.

Back to the Civil War memorabilia example, if you are selling old relics and items, you can link to someone who is an artist selling paintings of the period. Because people looking at your page may also be interested in the art, and vice versa, this will allow you to gain "Likes" from the other page, and allow the other page to in turn gain "Likes" from your page.

You can link to any related or non-related site, and agree with the other page to promote each other. You can ask them to point people to your page, and can do the same for them. This type of linking with other pages will give you the easy opportunity to gain "Likes" where you might have otherwise never found them.

Much of gaining likes can be based on luck, and linking with a variety of other pages will make sure that even if you are not the lucky page clicked, the eyes will still have a chance of seeing your page.

Creating Events

Creating an event on Facebook will give you an opportunity to alert all of your fans, followers, visitors, readers, customer and clients to any happenings that may be going on within your business.

Events are useful in making people aware of promotions, inviting people to open houses, getting people to events at your store, letting people know when things are happening, when objects are going on sale or when you will be providing services or making appearances.

To create an event, simply log onto your page, click onto your profile and click the small calendar on your publisher. The calendar is marked as a small page with a number 31 on it and can be found next to the links for video and photos.

The picture above displays your initial event options. When creating the event you must enter a title for your event. You can make this the name of the event, or a short description of what will be going on.

In addition to the name of the event, list the location in detail and be precise with the time. Use the drop-down tabs to indicate the day, month and time of your event, so readers know exactly when the happening will be going down.

Once you have entered the initial information for your event, click "Share" and you will be directed to the next page.

From this page, there is a myriad of details you can add to your event that will allow people to attend, RSVP, invite others and give them a clear idea of exactly what is going on. First, add details to the event. To do this, click "Edit this Event" on the right side of the page. This option will give you the opportunity to extensively alter the information about the event, going into great depth as to the details of the even.

You will be given an opportunity to make a tagline for the event, list a host, list the type of event, an ending time, make a description, tell the price and give detailed information on the location of the event and any necessary contact information.

Click "Save" once you have finished filling in your event's information and return to the event set up page.

You can add administrators to your event to allow others that you work with to alter the event details, control the RSVPs and invite others to the event.

By clicking "Invite People to Come" you can scroll through your list of contacts to pick people to send the invitation to.

The invitation will be sent as a link to your event and they will be able to either accept or decline your invitation, or indicate that they might be attending.

On your event page you can add videos or photographs, just as with your homepage and your wall, to promote and add interest to your event. You can also add links to give more information about your event and you can list the event as an open event, allowing your friends to add others to the event.

This gives you the opportunity to get people who are not on your friends list invited to your event.

An event is useful in getting actual interest in your event by promoting a real day and time when people can come and meet with you, view your products, hear about your services, purchase things or do a number of things that can help you to bring money to your business and will allow you to continue to generate profits.

With an event, you can invite thousands of followers, even those who do not follow you. An exciting event can compel them to follow you. You can also encourage followers who are attending the event to further invite their friends.

Using Notes and @replies

Notes and @replies can be another essential way of increasing your following. Notes are made to share large amounts of text with your followers, fans or visitors to your page and these can be made for a variety of reasons.

Whether you would like to make an announcement, share a speech or simply go on a rant, you can create a large text file and then simply tag all of your followers in the note. This will then appear on the page of each of your followers you have tagged and will be viewable by any other friends looking at their pages.

You can use the note to ask for "Likes" and others may jump on your page if what they see is interesting and exciting.

In addition to using notes, you can use @replies to draw attention to your page. These replies will allow you to post directly to someone else's page and you can encourage them to use an @reply on their page in references to your page.

While Facebook is an increasingly social network for the lives of people around the world, it is also now an indispensable business and marketing tool. "Likes" are leading the way in the trend of using Facebook for business pages and it is important to know how to squeeze the most out of the Facebook world.

These "Likes" can make or break your business and using these methods to add to your "Likes" will have your page among the most popular in your niche. One of the best free sources of advertising on the Web, Facebook also allows you to reach the biggest audience. Whether you "Like" it or not, getting those thumbs ups on Facebook are the way of the future.

Final Thoughts

Final Thoughts

Working with the top Internet Marketers who have contributed to this book has been a real honour and a pleasure. The information that they have revealed in these pages is incredibly valuable; both from a personal and business point of view.

To learn from their challenges, mistakes and successes is to compress years of learning the hard way, into a few hours of reading.

By reading this book, you have taken a step towards creating your own massive success. However, this alone is not anywhere near enough. To make true and lasting change in your life and set yourself on the path to great success, it will take more than a book or two.

The key to making a change in your life is you. And taking action! The best intentions in the world will amount to nothing if you do not take action. And you must invest in yourself. You must continue to keep learning, to expand your mind, to constantly seek out more knowledge and enlightenment.

Having read about the steps that the people in this book have taken to get where they are now, you should understand that there is no reason why you too cannot achieve such success.

To set your intention on what it is you want to achieve, you must begin by identifying your goals. Don't just think about it, sit down and put it on paper. Identify what you want to achieve this year, and next year and in five years and ten years. Be specific and then put that list somewhere where you will read it each and every day to set your intention in your mind. You will be amazed at the difference that this will make to your success in life. Better still get yourself a Coach! Someone whom you can share your goals with and then they'll keep you on track to fast tracking them.

Don't just put this book on shelf now that you have finished it. Look back over each chapter and ask yourself what you can you learn from it. Take notes on the most important messages you got out of each chapter. This will take a while, but it will be worth it. If you want good things to come to you then you must invest your time and energy into going out and chasing them.

The many bonuses in this book are your next step on the road to success. By going online and accessing them, you will be investing further in yourself and expanding your knowledge and learning even more. So what are you waiting for?

There's no better time in history than NOW to get started on using the internet as a vehicle to reach your financial & lifestyle dreams.

Business owners can now reach a level of advertising that was never before available and they can do it largely free or for a very small sum. Internet marketing allows businesses to generate profits through connection with a population of over 300,000,000 people and this connection can be had at the discretion of the business.

Since the early 2000s, Internet marketing has emerged as one of the true giants and dominant forces across the business world. It has become a new force in an enormous worldwide marketplace.

One last thing. Check out the valuable resource pages in the back of the book. The suppliers and website links are highly respected and sought after within the industry. So, give them a call or visit their websites for more information about their services.

We feel sure that you have enjoyed this book and that you have learnt some valuable lessons from it. Our hope for you now is that you step out and put this knowledge to use and take the next step on your journey towards awesome success in your life.

Live with passion!

David Lee, Darren Stephens & David Cavanagh

PS: *We'd love to hear and receive your letters or emails if you have been inspired by any of the stories in this book, so please contact us with your feedback or your own secrets to success*!

Email: info@GlobalPublishingGroup.com.au

About the Authors

David Lee

Growing up in his native Australia, David Lee migrated to the United Kingdom with his family in 1994. After working several years as an independent business systems consultant David fell into Internet Marketing by necessity back in 2004. It was by coincidence whilst attending his very first internet marketing conference in London that he met one of the presenters, and now co-author, David Cavanagh.

Working alongside successful property expert, Rick Otton, David was responsible for developing property cash flow systems that didn't require the buyer taking out a bank mortgage. In order to launch the concept and name "Rick Otton" into an initially sceptical British market it was a case of "sink or swim" for David to get the message out and then gain acceptance.

Swim he did as the reverberations have been felt around the UK due to David's persistence and determination to succeed against all odds! As a result David had to master a wide number of additional skills that includes online and offline marketing, mentoring, public speaking, copywriting, product launching and events management. It is this wide range of business life skills that David is recognised for, as well as already being an author himself.

David is the director of his Your Home Today Limited, using the creative methods for buying and selling of UK property that he helped develop. This is the practical side of allowing ordinary people to solve their property problems while the banking system fails them in today's financial climate.

With all the feverish attention of these new strategies, David also runs the educational arm of the business, known as Cash Flow Investor Limited. This is where the general public can learn from David's years of practical experience on how they can replicate the business model as a property investor, or even as a potential home buyer or seller that is frustrated or disillusioned with the traditional system.

Rather than having success go to his head, David still identifies with those having the same hunger and desire to succeed like he had back in 2004 by turning an idea into a way of life, and using the internet to help convey his message. It is widely recognised today in property circles that David's vision and achievements have lead to many of the changes that have taken place since then.

Most specialists can only talk on one topic of expertise, but David has spoken internationally on topics like Property Investing, Internet and Business Marketing, Personal Branding, Effective Communications and World Economics.

He lives in London with his wife Sabera and two children, Gerard and Adrian.

Darren Stephens

Entrepreneur, Author, Speaker and Business Consultant

Darren is a self-made multimillionaire and is a seasoned business executive, entrepreneur, growth strategist, bestselling author and consultant.

Darren was the founder and International Chairman of Mars Venus Coaching, one of the world's most respected and leading brands, and is now the Managing Director of global businesses such as Global Media Group and Successful Growth Strategies.

He is also a board member and International Marketing Director of the world's No# 1 eBay education company, Bidding Buzz Global Limited, with offices in 11 countries, including Australia, Rome, Paris, Singapore, Hong Kong, UK and North America.

He's recognised as an expert in the field of business development, sales and marketing, executive mentoring, franchising, international publishing, self-development and accelerated psychological transformation.

He is the author of 7 best-selling books such as "Top Franchise CEO's Secrets Revealed", "The 10 Day Turnaround, "The Success Principles" and "Our Internet Secrets," just to name a few. He was also the marketing genius behind developing the expansion of the Mars Venus brand, now in 150 countries and the books of which have been translated into 54 languages and have generated over a billion dollars in sales.

For more than 20 years, Darren has taught internationally, speaking to and motivating thousands of people in over 27 countries on how to create business, personal and financial success.

Darren's appearances on many television programs, and his articles published in newspapers and magazines nationally and internationally, has made him a sought-after speaker and consultant on the international stage.

Darren has also lectured at University on business management, marketing and psychological transformation and he is a certified Hypnotist, Neuro-Linguistic Programming (NLP) trainer and is qualified in Design Human Engineering and Time Line Therapy.

He is a fellow diplomat of the American Board of Hypnotherapy and a member of the International Franchise Association, Franchise Council of Australia National Speakers Association and is the founder of the prestigious Entrepreneurs Business School.

He lives in Melbourne, Australia, with his wife, Jackie, and their 7 children.

www.DarrenJStephens.com

David Cavanagh

David Cavanagh was born and raised in Sydney, Australia, growing up in a typical working class family. From the outset David was always inquisitive and wanting to discover new adventures that would be one of his greatest assets in later life.

David worked in the Staging Department at ATN-7 (Channel 7 TV) during the day, at the Sydney Opera House in the evening, while owning and managing the Disc Jockey Booking Centre in Sydney. He also worked in various sales related careers as well as practising massage and hypnosis as a registered practitioner. During this time David was married and had a daughter. Without realising it, the ups and downs of his business and married life would become the pillars of strength for David's foray into the world of Internet Marketing that followed years later. David was in desperate need of focus.

Like so many entrepreneurs who have faced adversity, such as a career and marriage that suffered and then failed, he had reached the point of no return in his life – it was time to either stagnate or move forward. It was only through his close friends who reached out to him that helped resurrect David and fulfill his potential with no holding back!

David was met by Mr Rob Bell at the World Internet Summit in 2004 and was given the opportunity to work full-time in Canada for 1ShoppingCart.com, promoting their online automation system on various stages of the World at major internet conferences. This was the catalyst where David had exposure to the quickly evolving world of online business marketing (and industry peers) and his adventurous childhood nature was rekindled.

Then came a sudden change in David's life - he decided to change his environment and moved away from the cold Canadian winters to the balmy temperatures of Thailand (where he still lives today). David was referred to as the "World's Number One Internet Newbies Coach" at nearly every internet marketing seminar he presented and he wanted to keep that momentum and image going for many years to come.

David remarried in Thailand and has a beautiful Thai wife, 3 daughters and has embraced the beautiful Thai culture as well. David worked tirelessly to build his business from the ground up, now owning the most successful internet training program with an international team of trainers and coaches who support him tirelessly. So successful has this metamorphosis been that David's courses and programs are regularly sold out with attendees coming from across the globe to train personally with him.

This first book collaboration represents another milestone in David's career. You the reader are now a direct beneficiary of this. What you'll find included in this book is a result of much trial and error testing so you can succeed online.

David resides in Pattaya, Thailand with his wife Wanna, their children Di and Fahsai, and his married daughter Krystal living on the Gold Coast in Australia. He runs a 52 week internet coaching program, and his 12 day Best Coaching Program workshops are run in Pattaya should you consider being trained in person by David and his team at one of his World renowned international workshops.

www.BestCoachingProgram.com

Recommended
Success Resources

Websites

Darren Stephens	www. DarrenJStephens.com
David Cavanagh	www.DavidCavanagh.com
David Cavanagh's Internet Coaching Workshops	http://www davidcavanaghworkshops.com/
Publishing & online ebooks	www.TheGlobalPublishingGroup.com
How To Write A Best Selling Book	www.HowToWriteABestseller.com
Private Label products	www.UnselfishMarketer.com/Discount
FusionHQ software	www.FusionHQ.com/package/internet-secrets-revealed-book
Facebook ebook	www.darrenjstephens.com/facebook-marketing-secrets/
Business & Marketing tips	www.The10DayTurnaround.com
Ebay	www.Ebay.com
Ebay resources & tips	www.BiddingBuzz.com
Elance	www.elance.com/
Odesk	www.odesk.com/
AWeber	www.aweber.com/
Yahoo Answers	www.answers.yahoo.com/
Ezine Articles	www.ezinearticles.com/
Webwire	www.webwire.com/
Facebook	www.facebook.com
Myspace	www.myspace.com/
Linkedin	www.linkedin.com/
Google Analytics	www.google.com/analytics/
Google	www.google.com/

Lightning Source UK Ltd.
Milton Keynes UK
UKOW030356080312

188515UK00001B/11/P